A Christmas Gift

From

Dr. and Mrs. J. Victor Eagan

and

Eagan Orthodontics, P.C. Staff

December 2004

"In a straightforward, easy-to-read, and profound way, the Eagans reveal the priceless, practical, biblical principles necessary for high achievement, personal happiness, and business success."

— WILLARD THEISSEN, FOUNDER AND HOST,
It's a New Day, CHRISTIAN TELEVISION SHOW, NOW TV, CANADA

"A riveting, timeless, literary work. Biblically-sound, it should be required reading for every Christian. This book is vital for discovering your God-given purpose and achieving unparalleled success."

— RICARDO M. MARTIN, FOUNDER AND PUBLISHER,
CHRISTIAN COVENANT NEWSPAPERS, MICHIGAN

"Revolutionary, practical and powerful wisdom to get into God's perfect will for your life. It challenges people of every age and all walks of life to step into their personal greatness and realize their God-given potential."

— BISHOP GEORGE L. DAVIS, SENIOR PASTOR,
FAITH CHRISTIAN CENTER, FLORIDA

"Bound to be a classic — *How to Discover Your Purpose in 10 Days* brings a unique depth and practicality to the teaching on purpose. Engaging, profound, and filled with rich, vivid examples, the Eagans give insight from their personal life experiences in discovering and operating successfully in God's perfect will."

— PASTORS BEN & JEWEL TANKARD,
SENIOR PASTORS AND FOUNDERS, DESTINY CENTER, TENNESSEE

"Using pragmatic examples, the Eagans masterfully minister the Word of God in answering one of life's most fundamental and perplexing questions: 'What on earth am I here for?' Essential for everyone who wants to discover God's plan for their lives!"

— AL HOLLINGSWORTH, PRESIDENT AND CEO,
ALDELANO PACKAGING CORPORATION, CALIFORNIA

"Truly a work of God! This anointed, brilliant, and easy-to-understand book will change your life. After the Eagans taught these principles to my staff, our office was transformed. Not only did people develop a greater appreciation and love for their jobs, our profitability soared and our productivity went to greater heights!"

— DR. BARRY RUSSELL, PRESIDENT AND CEO,
LOFTANN ENTERPRISES, LIMITED, NASSAU, BAHAMAS

How to Discover Your PURPOSE *in* 10 Days

Other Books Authored by the Eagans Include:

Dominating Business
How to Prosper on Your Job

Anointed for Work
Using the Tools from Sunday to Succeed on Monday

How to Determine Your Motivational Gift
Learn How God Wired You

Dominating Money
Personal Financial Intelligence

The Character of Success
26 Characteristics of Highly Successful People

The Word @ Work, Volumes I & II
Scriptures for the Workplace

How to Discover Your Purpose in 10 Days
Self-Assessment Workbook

How to Discover Your Purpose in 10 Days
Prayers and Daily Journal

Upcoming Books Include:

Godly Leadership in the Workplace

The Road to the Wealthy Place
Dominating Money in Business

Terminating Conflict
God's Solutions to Resolving Conflict Permanently

All titles are available on-line at www.eaganbooks.com.
Also available: CDs and DVDs.
For more information, E-mail us at info@eaganbooks.com
or call 1-877-EAGANS1 (324-2671).

How to Discover Your PURPOSE *in* 10 Days

God's Path *to a* Full *and* Satisfied Life

Dr. J. Victor and
Catherine B. Eagan

WORKPLACE
WISDOM

WORKPLACE
WISDOM

SOUTHFIELD, MICHIGAN 48076 USA

How to Discover Your Purpose in 10 Days: God's Path to a Full and Satisfied Life

Workplace Wisdom Publishing, LLC.,
17600 W. 12 Mile Road, Suite 1, Southfield, Michigan 48076
www.workplacewisdompublishing.com • www.eaganbooks.com • 1-877-EAGANS1 (324-2671)

Publisher's Cataloging-in-Publication Data
(Prepared by The Donohue Group, Inc.)

Eagan, J. Victor.
How to discover your purpose in 10 days : God's path to a full and satisfied life / J. Victor and Catherine B. Eagan.
p. ; cm.
ISBN: 1-932477-00-4
1. Self-actualization (Psychology) 2. Spiritual life. I. Eagan, Catherine B. II. Title. III. Title: How to discover your purpose in ten days

BF637.S4 E141 2004 2004110720
158.1

Printed on acid-free paper.

Cover Design by Brand Navigation — Bill Chiaravalle, Terra Petersen. www.brandnavigation.com
Interior Design by Pneuma Books, LLC. www.pneumabooks.com

Printed in the United States of America.

09 08 07 06 05 10 9 8 7 6 5 4 3 2 1

DEDICATION

This book is dedicated to Mrs. Louise Eagan and Mrs. Adele Helen Cartey, our mothers, who understood the gifts God created each of us to be. While raising us, they overcame many obstacles and made sacrifices to ensure that we would reach our God-given potential. They nurtured, encouraged, and allowed us to flow in our purpose to the glory of God; and for that, we are eternally grateful.

Also, to every person who is in search of purpose and to those who are in search of their God-given greatness to the glory of God.

Table of Contents

PURPOSE
FOREWORD

Foreword

The greatest tragedy in life is not death, but life without a purpose. It is more tragic to be alive and not know why than to be dead and not know life. Without purpose life has no meaning and existence has no reason, therefore, the greatest discovery in life is the discovery of personal purpose and destiny. The most important thing in life is the pursuit and fulfillment of that purpose. Therefore, knowledge and understanding of the processes that lead to its fulfillment are critical and must be the concern of every individual.

There is no greater discovery than the discovery of personal purpose. The discovery of purpose is the heart of life and the revelation that gives life meaning and value. Without purpose life has no relevance and time has no reason. What is purpose? Purpose is defined as the original reason for the creation of a thing — the original intent for the existence of a thing. In essence, purpose is why a product was created. Purpose is the end for which the means exists. Thus, purpose is the only true source of meaning and fulfillment in life.

For many years now I have taught, counseled, and researched the subject of purpose and its meaning to millions of people; and I am convinced that until an individual discovers a sense of purpose and destiny in their lives, living is nothing but an aimless experiment in daily frustration. I also contend that most anti-social behavior, violent crime, and substance abuse is a direct result of the absence of a sense of purpose in the lives of members of our societies. The discovery of a sense of purpose and destiny produces a spirit of responsibility, discipline, and order in life.

It is said that the poorest man in the world is the man without a dream. If this is true, then the most frustrated man in the world is the man with a dream that never becomes a reality. Knowing the end of a journey but not knowing the way to get there is an exercise in disillusionment. We all need help in getting to the end of our dream and arriving at our destiny. In essence we need a plan, a life map.

Dr. Victor and Catherine Eagan in *How to Discover Your Purpose in 10 Days* provide the missing link to knowing your dream and its fulfillment. The content of this work is imperative for the individual who wants to achieve his or her ultimate goals in life. Victor and Catherine with their simple, yet profound approach to this most important subject provide practical steps and easy-to-understand principles as an action plan to identify, discover, understand, explore, and take you on a journey to find and fulfill your purpose. The authors leap over complicated theoretical and philosophical jargon to present user-friendly concepts anyone can apply. Their progressive line-upon-line delivery of action-oriented directions for the reader is like a manual for life.

How to Discover Your Purpose in 10 Days is a natural and excellent companion book to my earlier published work, *In Pursuit of*

Purpose, and provides the next step in the process of fulfilling your personal and corporate purpose.

I recommend the work highly and believe it will be the key to filling the gap between knowing your purpose and destiny and getting there. Everyone who desires to live a full life, maximize their potential, and make a lasting impact on their generation will find this book a necessary part of the process. Read each page and peel the wisdom from every paragraph. The wisdom contained in this book will take you leap years forward to your dream and save you many unnecessary mistakes and regrets through the process.

How to Discover Your Purpose in 10 Days will become a classic in the lives of thousands of purpose-driven people and a must for every library. Open these pages, read with an open mind, embrace the practical principles, and take action today. If you do, I'll see you at the end of your dream.

Dr. Victor and Catherine Eagan have been personal friends for many years, and I can attest to their passion and commitment to helping you and others pursue their God-given assignment in life and fill the earth with their purpose. Their personal accomplishments and purpose-directed lives are prototypes of the principles in this book. The subject of purpose has been a critical part of my ministry for over thirty years, and I know that the Eagans are qualified to address this topic with much authority. I commend this work to you without reservation.

DR. MYLES MUNROE, CEO AND PRESIDENT
BFM GROUP OF COMPANIES

PURPOSE

PREFACE

Preface

For over fifteen years we have traveled across the United States, Canada, and around the world teaching biblical principles in the areas of business and finance. In doing so, we discovered a great tragedy, namely that the vast majority of people do not know their purpose. Either that or they have hit a ceiling in the search for significance. Knowing one's purpose is fundamental to pleasing God and having a full life here on earth.

Our heart is to see people get into their purpose and fulfill their God-given destiny. We have encountered people from all walks of life — rich and poor, believers and unbelievers, workers and the unemployed — and among them we have observed a common thread which gave rise to our deep-felt passion. That thread was that an exceptional few understood their purpose. This provoked us to deep study, endless prayer, and revelation from God on the matter.

That desire led to an anointing from God to teach people *how* to get into their purpose and live the good life that He preordained before the foundation of the earth. Thousands have come to know their purpose through our teachings and have prospered in their families, relationships, workplaces, businesses, and finances. It is our greatest desire that you will be added to that number.

Both of us have been tremendously blessed by God. As children, we knew what we were called and assigned to do on earth. While our stories are individually different, there are common denominators — purpose known, obstacles overcome by God's grace, and fulfillment realized through operating in the perfect will of God for our lives.

We wrote *How to Discover Your Purpose in 10 Days* to empower every person to get into their purpose and to excel to such heights that God's glory might be seen on His children as they rule and reign with Him in this life. The gifts and calling of God are without repentance. God's gifts inside of you are inexhaustible.

How to Discover Your Purpose in 10 Days was written under a precious anointing from the Holy Spirit to help you seek God, learn your gifts, develop your talents, understand how He wired you, and fulfill your destiny.

We have prayed for you and we know that as you are faithful to read each day's lesson, pray, and complete the action plans using the *Self-Assessment Workbook* and the *Prayers and Daily Journal,* God will show Himself and you will be blessed. (Jeremiah 29:11)

God is expecting to give you a great end,

The Eagans

WORKPLACE
WISDOM

Acknowledgments

WE WOULD LIKE TO THANK:

Our Heavenly Father, for anointing and calling us to our purpose
Each other, for always supporting, loving, and encouraging one another
Our parents, whose love, prayers, and guidance inspired us
Our spiritual parents, Bishop Keith A. Butler and Minister Deborah Butler
And other gifted people whose dedication helped us write this book:
Bill Gothard, Institute in Basic Life Principles
Marilyn Hickey, Marilyn Hickey Ministries
Don and Katie Fortune, Authors
Dr. Myles Munroe, Chairman,
International Third World Leaders Association
Starra Pollard, our Executive Assistant
Lauren Doyle-Davis, our Personal Assistant
Pneuma Books, LLC, our Interior Designers
Brand Navigation, LLC, our Graphic Artists

PURPOSE

INTRODUCTION

Introduction

Welcome to *How to Discover Your Purpose in 10 Days: God's Path to a Full and Satisfied Life.* This is a special edition of the purpose seminar that my wife and I have been teaching throughout the nation for the past decade. We are honored that God has given us the privilege of sharing fundamental principles for finding and fulfilling your purpose, and we are excited that you will be joining us on a 10-day journey to discovering God's plan for your life.

This system works. Read the teaching and complete the action plans and self-assessments that accompany each lesson. Use the *Prayers and Daily Journal* to write down your thoughts each day. We promise that if you diligently and prayerfully complete the 10-day process, God will begin to reveal to you His plans, desires, and purpose for your life.

There is nothing worse than wandering aimlessly in life, never reaching your full potential. God's best is for you to have success. This is possible when you walk in the fullness of what He has for you. God designed you to do great and mighty exploits on earth; and we pray that as you complete these 10 days you will begin to walk in the greatness that He preordained for you before the foundation of the world.

The material is life changing and it will be the same for you as it has been for countless others throughout the years. We are extremely excited for you! Our prayer is that God will reveal His specific purpose for your life and you will excel to the glory of God.

HOW TO USE THIS BOOK

How to Discover Your Purpose in 10 Days is designed to help you facilitate and identify your purpose. We as Christians are often told that God has a purpose for our lives; yet for many it is difficult to determine what that is. There are three types of people: those who do not know their God-given purpose; those who know their purpose, but are underdeveloped in it; and those who know their purpose, are developing it, and maturing.

No matter what stage of life you may be in right now, this book is for you!

How to Discover Your Purpose in 10 Days is a step-by-step, simple, yet comprehensive way to identify who God made you to be. It is an exciting journey to once and for all discover the greatness within you that God had in mind when He formed you in your mother's womb.

> Before I formed you in the womb I knew you; before you were born I sanctified you; I ordained you a prophet to the nations.
>
> JEREMIAH 1:5 (NKJV)

How to Discover Your Purpose in 10 Days is designed to propel you to new heights and teach you how to fulfill the perfect will of God for your life.

THE GOAL OF THE BOOK

The goal of *How to Discover Your Purpose in 10 Days* is to be a conduit in helping you understand your God-given, unique life assignment and unlock your personal greatness. At the same time, the book will help you feel good about yourself by helping you to understand yourself and others, including your family, your co-workers, children, boss, and friends.

The book is designed incrementally; and each day builds upon the other. To obtain the maximum results from the program it is strongly recommended that you undertake it day by day, prayerfully. With great excitement and anticipation we pray that after the 10 days have been completed, you will discover your purpose and begin to walk in God's best for your life.

THE STRUCTURE

How to Discover Your Purpose in 10 Days is designed so that each day takes you further along the pathway to discovering your God-given life purpose. As you prayerfully read and complete the associated exercises, you will begin to tap into the greatness within you.

Day 1: Discovering the Greatness Within

Day 1 marks the beginning of the exciting 10-day journey to your pathway to purpose. Day 1 reveals many of the awesome reasons why it is vitally important to identify and realize your God-given destiny.

Day 2: The Pathway to Discover Your Purpose — The Formative Years

In Day 2, you will discover how your purpose is intricately and progressively revealed to you by God. Even as a young child, your interests, natural talents, and abilities reflect the greatness God placed on the inside of you before birth. You were elaborately and intricately fashioned in the image of God Almighty and He formed you with a magnificent destiny in mind.

Day 3: Narrowing Your Focus — Young Adulthood

Day 3 focuses on the importance of determining your ruling passion and allowing it to govern your decisions on education, training, activities, and jobs that you undertake during young adulthood. God placed a ruling passion in you that reflects your innermost being. Uncovering your ruling passion is pivotal in discovering your God-given purpose.

Day 4: Obstacles on the Pathway to Purpose

Day 4 is the day of breakthrough! It reveals many of the obstacles that may arise along your pathway to purpose. There are countless reasons why you may get diverted, distracted, or thwarted from your pathway to purpose. Day 4 helps you locate yourself, make the necessary adjustments, and begin operating in your purpose.

Day 5: God's Unique Motivational Gifts — Introduction/Perceiver

In Day 5, the motivational gifts are introduced and the motivational gift of the Perceiver is discussed. God has called the Perceiver to intercede on the behalf of others and distinguish between right and wrong.

Day 6: God's Unique Motivational Gifts — Server/Teacher

In Day 6, the motivational gifts of Server and Teacher are revealed.

God has called the Server to perform the practical needs of others, while the Teacher has been anointed by God to manage and disseminate information.

Day 7: God's Unique Motivational Gifts — Exhorter/Giver

In Day 7, the motivational gifts of Exhorter and Giver are uncovered. God has called the Exhorter to encourage and build people up, while the Giver has been anointed by God to mobilize resources for the aid and benefit of others.

Day 8: God's Unique Motivational Gifts — Administrator/Compassion

In Day 8, the motivational gifts of Administrator and Compassion are outlined. God has called the Administrator to facilitate, administrate, and organize, while the Compassion gift is anointed by God to attend to and care for the emotional needs of others. Day 8 also answers the questions and challenges often faced in attempting to narrow down your motivational gift.

Day 9: Maturing in Your Purpose — The Adult Years

By Day 9, you should have begun to discover your God-given purpose. With this exciting revelation, you will learn how important it is to become more developed and mature in your purpose. It is God's desire that you dominate to His glory in your vocation. To do this, you must mature in your life work. Not only will you please God, you will also live a satisfied and fulfilled life.

Day 10: Fulfilling the Greatness Within

There is a great life work that the Lord is counting on you to fulfill. There is also an awesome destiny that God has prepared before the foundation of the world for you to realize. So, this power-packed series concludes on Day 10 centering on how to make your purpose a reality in your life.

You were fearfully and wonderfully made by God and He placed greatness on the inside of you before you were born. You have been called of God to do great and mighty exploits on earth and Day 10 reveals steps that will empower and enable you to soar in your life purpose.

Invite God to Help You

We suggest that prior to beginning each day of purpose that you pray and invite God to help you get revelation, knowledge, and understanding concerning the important information you are about to receive.

> Wisdom is the principal thing; Therefore get wisdom. And in all your getting, get understanding. PROVERBS 4:7 (NKJV)

We pray,

> That the God of our Lord Jesus Christ, the Father of glory, may give to you the spirit of wisdom and revelation in the knowledge of Him, the eyes of your understanding being enlightened; that you may know what is the hope of His calling, what are the riches of the glory of His inheritance in the saints, and what is the exceeding greatness of His power toward us who believe, according to the working of His mighty power.
>
> EPHESIANS 1:17-19 (NKJV)

Next, prepare your heart and mind in Christ Jesus. Earnestly seek understanding about how He created you and the unique purpose He planned for you to fulfill on earth — your special assignment, your life purpose.

> But without faith it is impossible to please Him, for he who comes to God must believe that He is, and that He is a rewarder of those who diligently seek Him.
>
> HEBREWS 11:6 (NKJV)

When you see this icon, turn to either your *Self-Assessment Workbook* or *Prayers and Daily Journal* as instructed for additional exercises and activities.

Then, read each day's material, listen to the teaching, and complete the action plans and self-assessments that correspond to each day. They are designed to help you focus, identify areas for change, and receive the maximum benefit from the book.

Journal each day in your *Prayers and Daily Journal* and be careful not to overlook the small bits of information. Remember, we are carefully working on a puzzle that God has masterfully designed — you. So don't let any of the pieces get lost.

Purpose each day to embrace who God made you to be. Don't begrudge your uniqueness or belittle your importance. You are a royal priesthood and your contribution is important to the establishment of God's kingdom on earth. Know that He is depending on you to fulfill your purpose.

> But you are a chosen generation, a royal priesthood, a holy nation, His own special people, that you may proclaim the praises of Him who called you out of darkness into His marvelous light. 1 PETER 2:9 (NKJV)

What is required of you is time, discipline, and commitment.

Lastly, be mindful that 10 days is a short period of time to resolve two of life's most fundamental and perplexing questions — Who am I? And what on earth am I here for? Our goal is to get you on the path to discovering your purpose. It can be the beginning of one of the best journeys of your Christian life.

Remember, *God* is expecting greatness from your life.

May the Lord richly bless you as you discover your purpose.

The Eagans

WORKPLACE
WISDOM

It is impossible to do everything people want you to do. You have just enough time to do God's will. Purpose-driven living leads to a simpler lifestyle and saner schedule. RICK WARREN

A difficult time can be more readily endured if we retain the conviction that our existence holds a purpose — a cause to pursue, a person to love, a goal to achieve. JOHN MAXWELL

Outstanding people have one thing in common: an absolute sense of mission. ZIG ZIGLAR

The masterpiece of man is to live to the purpose.

BENJAMIN FRANKLIN

Multitudes of people, drifting aimlessly to and fro without a set purpose, deny themselves such fulfillment of their capacities, and the satisfying happiness which attends it. They are not wicked, they are only shallow. They are not mean or vicious; they simply are empty — shake them and they would rattle like gourds. They lack range, depth, and conviction. Without purpose their lives ultimately wander into the morass of dissatisfaction. As we harness our abilities to a steady purpose and undertake the long pull toward its accomplishment, rich compensations reward us. A sense of purpose simplifies life and therefore concentrates our abilities; and concentration adds power. KENNETH HILDEBRAND

Singleness of purpose is one of the chief essentials for success in life, no matter what may be one's aim.

JOHN D. ROCKEFELLER

There is one quality which one must possess to win, and that is definiteness of purpose, the knowledge of what one wants, and a burning desire to possess it. NAPOLEON HILL

PURPOSE

DAY ONE

Day 1 marks the beginning of the exciting 10-day journey to your pathway to purpose. Day 1 reveals many of the awesome reasons why it is vitally important to identify and realize your God-given destiny. You will also learn about the hidden problems of never discovering and fulfilling your life purpose.

1

DAY ONE

Discovering the Greatness Within

It is God's best for us to operate in our purpose and fulfill His master plan for our lives. Many great men and women have lost their way because they didn't know their purpose. We know there is greatness inside of you and are excited about the awesome things the Lord shall reveal to you as you begin this 10-day journey to discovering your purpose. Let us look at someone who lost their way.

THE TRAGEDY OF NOT KNOWING YOUR PURPOSE

As our wedding day drew near we were very excited about the life God had in store for us. All the plans were ready and it was just days away. For some reason we began to reflect on the people we knew, wondering if all six hundred invited guests would show up. While reviewing the guest list, we came across the name of a prominent dentist and paused in deep reflection.

This man was a highly successful dentist with a large practice, overseeing multiple dentists in his office. In fact, he was one of the first African-American dentists in our area to develop a large multi-dentist practice in a high-rise building. Outwardly he had all the trappings of success. He was highly respected in the community, drove a fancy car, and had a lovely residence. Yet, we were saddened because we knew he was very confused.

He had graduated from college, professional dental school, and he had also earned a professional master's degree in business science — a total of twenty-two years of schooling and over a half million dollars in educational expenses. He had been divorced twice and he was the father of beautiful children. Still he was desperately in search of his purpose. He never seemed to be satisfied — always feeling that his greatness was hidden. He felt that he was trying too hard, never really fitting in, always pretending. The outer projection and essence of his personality was vastly compromised. Although he was a Christian, he was constantly asking these questions: What am I here for? What is the meaning for my life? Is this all there is to life? He struggled with not being satisfied with his degrees, or his titles, or his money, or his career, or his reputation. Sadly, he was not even satisfied with his relationship with God.

As we continued to talk, we prayed for him and moved on to more exciting thoughts about our wedding day. It was a fabulous day and God's hand was to be seen everywhere. Almost six hundred people came to celebrate our marriage and it was a glorious day. Somehow, through all the festivities, we noticed that we did not see the dentist, but we thought nothing of it. We left Michigan for a three-and-a-half week honeymoon.

About two weeks into our trip we called home to check in. Among all the great reports there was one that was terribly disturbing. We learned that the dentist had committed suicide the day after our wedding. What a tragedy! A godless, senseless, act.

For the rest of our honeymoon, we pondered how this could happen to a man, who in everyone's eyes, was a leader in his industry, a successful businessman, and had all the trappings of success. It was extremely difficult to understand how he could look at his life and say, "Life is not worth living anymore." But he felt that his life had neither purpose nor significance; and that because the greatness he felt within could not be expressed, he took his life.

It was said that the last straw was an impending business deal — the selling of a major asset to get more cash flow. He had convinced himself that it would never sell. The next morning, after he killed himself, the asset sold before anyone found out that he had died. He was tricked out of fulfilling his purpose.

By deceiving this dentist into believing that his life was meaningless and purposeless, Satan was able to steal his purpose. Satan's design is to take you off track, off your pathway, and to steal the greatness inside of you. But it shall not be so with you. Remember, Jesus Christ overcame Satan through the Blood of the Lamb.

> Little children, you are of God [you belong to Him] and have [already] defeated and overcome them [the agents of the antichrist], because He Who lives in you is greater (mightier) than he who is in the world.
>
> 1 JOHN 4:4 (AMP)

Our prayer for you is that Satan will never steal your purpose.

The Graveyard Is Full of Unfulfilled Purpose

We have heard it said the richest place on earth is the cemetery. The graveyard is rich with great God-inspired dreams, inventions, books, masterpieces, businesses and ministries that could have changed the course of the world, but instead went to the grave. Purpose and destiny are designed for life, not death.

Many people have no clue why God placed them here on earth, but they do not go so far as to commit suicide. The dentist account is a stark example of what not knowing your purpose can do. You see, it is purpose which strikes at the reason for being. Without knowing your purpose, one can aimlessly wander through life, all the time knowing deep inside that there is greatness to be realized; yet it continues to cry out for its release.

Problems with Not Knowing Your Purpose

Not knowing your purpose presents enormous problems. The principal one is that if you do not know your purpose, you will not honor God. Also, you will drift through life dissatisfied with yourself and feel unfulfilled.

Further complications include:

- Depression
- Lack of contentment and fulfillment in your family life, on the job, and socially resulting in varying levels of abuse
- Rebellion against parents, authorities, and bosses
- Lack of self-appreciation and respect
- Low self-esteem
- Premature death and/or aging
- Lazy and lackadaisical attitude
- Inability to be successful
- Underachievement
- Financial instability

Although many of us have faced one or more of these problems, we must recognize that often, such issues affect us because of our lack of understanding concerning our God-given purpose. If we fully understood it, we would handle setbacks and problems with an understanding that no matter what obstacles arise, we have been made conquerors through Jesus Christ and therefore are assured of a victorious outcome.

> But thanks be to God, Who gives us the victory [making us conquerors] through our Lord Jesus Christ.
>
> 1 CORINTHIANS 15:57 (AMP)

THERE IS GREATNESS ON THE INSIDE OF YOU

God puts greatness within us as a demonstration of Himself. God is great and we are made in His likeness, so He has made us great. Each one of His creations is unique, equipped, and designed with gifts and attributes necessary to carry out His plans for their life. The gifts God gives us are without repentance, which means He does not take them away or change His mind about having given them. Everything we need to be successful, receive the highest rewards, and experience the greatest hours of our lives, God has already placed inside of us.

> I will praise You, for I am fearfully and wonderfully made;
> Marvelous are Your works, And that my soul knows very well.
>
> PSALM 139:14 (NKJV)

Purpose Engenders Greatness

If you know and are operating in your life purpose, others will see greatness manifested in every area of your life. You will be energetic, purposeful, and excited about your work and life. You will receive pleasure and immense satisfaction from doing God's will for your life. Not only will you benefit by walking in the fullness of what God has called you to do, others will also be affected greatly by someone who is passionate and highly talented.

Conversely, those who are not in their God-given purpose view their work and life as menial, tedious, and unfulfilling.

Consider these essential questions people ask regarding the search for fulfillment and significance:

- Why do I exist?
- What am I called to do with my life?
- What is my purpose in life?
- What can I do to bring meaning and significance to my life?

Here is a fundamental truth for you to contemplate:

> *True fulfillment in life is directly related to realizing that God created you to perform a specific purpose. Your purpose is manifested in your life work and life service to others. You become fulfilled by performing to the best of your God-given ability.*

KNOWING YOUR PURPOSE SETS YOU FREE TO SOAR

When you know your purpose it becomes clear why you are the way you are, why you think the way you think, and why you do things the way you do them. You begin to have an appreciation of yourself and an even greater appreciation for God who marvelously created and designed you.

The Benefits of Knowing Your Purpose

When we invest time and money in an endeavor, we want to know the rewards. The benefits listed here are just a few reasons why it is important to take the time necessary to discover your purpose.

- You will have a full and satisfied life
- You will enjoy life and feel good about yourself

- You will feel as though your life really makes a difference
- You will be content
- Your job and career will become more enjoyable
- You will have a more stable marriage and better understanding of your spouse
- You will waste less time and energy engaged in unproductive activities
- You will feel greater fulfillment because you know you are performing God's will and purpose for your life
- You will be able to enjoy and get more pleasure out of life
- Your level of personal satisfaction, confidence, and significance will soar
- You will stop feeling like you're wandering aimlessly through life
- You will be able to take control of your life and make your dreams a reality
- You will unlock and fulfill the greatness within
- You will maximize your strengths and minimize your weaknesses
- You will become comfortable with who you are
- You will have great relationships with virtually no jealousy, envy, or strife, knowing you are not in competition but are a complement in every relationship
- You will understand what makes you and others tick
- Your life will become an expression of how God made you
- You will be able to strengthen and mature in your natural gifts and talents, thereby making you more successful, valuable, and profitable
- You will operate in the highest level of anointing
- The greatest reward is you please God

What Is Purpose?

Let's consider what Dr. Myles Munroe, an internationally known author and pastor, has to say about purpose.

> Purpose is the original intent for the creation of a thing.
> Purpose is the original reason for the existence of a thing.
> Purpose is the cause for the creation of a thing.
> It is the desired result that initiates production.
> It is the need that makes a manufacturer produce a specific product.
>
> It is a destination that prompts the journey.
> It is the end for which the reason and the means exist.
> It is purpose that gives everything meaning.
> Without purpose, life is an experiment or haphazard journey.
> Without purpose, life is subjective, it is a trial and error gained that is ruled by chance and circumstances.
> Without purpose, time has no meaning.
> Without purpose, energy has no reason.
> Without purpose, life has no precision.[1]

GOD MADE EVERYTHING WITH A PURPOSE

When we are introduced to God in Genesis 1:1, God is creating with purpose and intent. We see God creating the heavens and the earth, the light and the darkness, the divide to separate the waters and to create dry land.

> In the beginning God created the heavens and the earth.
>
> GENESIS 1:1 (NKJV)

> Thus says God the LORD, Who created the heavens and stretched them out, Who spread forth the earth and that which comes from it, Who gives breath to the people on it, And spirit to those who walk on it. ISAIAH 42:5 (NKJV)

We see Him providing solutions to the challenges that present themselves, creating light to meet a future need.

> Then God said, "Let there be light"; and there was light.
> GENESIS 1:3 (NKJV)

God Created Man with a Purpose

Before God created man, He put purpose in his heart. He created the environment and all its resources and then God waited until all the conditions were perfect and He made man. This was a divine, ultimate act. It was so sacred to God that He fashioned man after Himself. What an honor! There is nothing else in heaven or earth that God created which is in His own image.

Finally, God performed the divine by breathing the breath of life into man, and man became a living soul.

> Then God said, "Let Us make man in Our image, according to Our likeness; let them have dominion over the fish of the sea, over the birds of the air, and over the cattle, over all the earth and over every creeping thing that creeps on earth."
> GENESIS 1:26 (NKJV)

Before You Were Born, God Had Your Assignment

While man was yet in the mind of God, He gave him his assignment. Assignment precedes creation. Therefore, what you are to become — or your purpose — is predetermined. Before you were born, God had your assignment in place. Your birth was a glorious day and the beginning of your destiny.

> Before I formed you in the womb I knew [and] approved of you [as My chosen instrument], and before you were born I separated and set you apart, consecrating you; [and] I appointed you as a prophet to the nations.
>
> JEREMIAH 1:5 (AMP)

Notice that God ordained Jeremiah to be a prophet before Jeremiah was born. Likewise, before you were born, God had you on His mind. God knew exactly what He was creating and assigning each of us to become before we were ever born.

Most people do not have a revelation of the fact that God has preordained a specific purpose for their lives. Thus, they don't seek God's plan and will or tap into their inner greatness.

EVEN OBJECTS HAVE PURPOSE

Every object is produced for a specific reason. It exists for its purpose. Success is obtained only when performing the purpose for which it was created. Consider these objects and their purpose:

- Glass — to hold liquid
- Napkin — to wipe things
- Microphone — to project voice into the air or onto a recording device
- Chair — to support a person in a seated position
- Pen — to write
- Clothes — to keep warm, to cover nakedness
- Car, train, and plane — for transportation

KNOWING YOUR PURPOSE IS THE STAIRWAY TO SUCCESS

You will have limited success in a purpose for which you were not created. When you operate outside of your God-given purpose, you will feel awkward, be unfulfilled, or not completely realize the awesome destiny God had in mind when He fashioned you.

You must find your unique purpose. There are a variety of purposes, so yours may not be the same as your parents, your siblings, and others. It may have some similar components, but be tailored to you.

GOD HAS PROVIDED THE GOOD LIFE FOR US IN ADVANCE

God prearranged a life for you to live and it is your job to seek it out. He is not hiding it from you; you just have to get into agreement with God.

Until you tap into your God-given gifts, talents, and assignments, you will not reach your full potential. Most people come and go in this life and never fulfill the plan of God for their life. This is why so many people are discontent—saved and unsaved alike. It is only when you recognize God's master design for your life that you will have full contentment and mastery.

> For we are God's [own] handiwork (His workmanship), recreated in Christ Jesus, [born anew] that we may do those good works which God predestined (planned beforehand) for us [taking paths which He prepared ahead of time], that we should walk in them [living the good life which He prearranged and made ready for us to live].
>
> EPHESIANS 2:10 (AMP)

You may feel like others have a special purpose, but you don't. However, the Bible tells us that God is no respecter of persons, meaning He does not discriminate — we are all set apart for a special use. He longs for you to embrace your assignment. You may be called to be a teacher, secretary, politician, minister, business mogul, or homemaker, but there is something that you are anointed and gifted to do.

MAKE SURE YOUR PLANS ARE GOD'S PLANS

We as believers want to make sure that we are seeking God's plans so that He can make them sure — established. God is under no obligation to bless, anoint, finance, or further the plans of man. This is why so many believers get into trouble. They develop their own plans and prayerfully expect God's support. When success does not come they blame God, while all the time God is nudging them on the inside to go in another direction so He can make them established.

> A man's mind plans his way, but the Lord directs his steps and makes them sure. PROVERBS 16:9 (AMP)

> Roll your works upon the Lord [commit and trust them wholly to Him; He will cause your thoughts to become agreeable to His will, and] so shall your plans be established and succeed. PROVERBS 16:3 (AMP)

FAITH IS REQUIRED

It takes faith to accept and believe that God created you with a specific purpose. Secular humanists do not believe that the world was created by Jehovah God as Christians do. Instead, they believe that man is his own god. They believe in evolution, which purports that the world and its inhabitants were created by a random sequence of events and natural selection, commonly known as the Big Bang Theory. These individuals believe that life is an experiment and there is no preordained purpose for their lives.

> But without faith it is impossible to please and be satisfactory to Him. For whoever would come near to God must [necessarily] believe that God exists and that He is the rewarder of those who earnestly and diligently seek Him [out].
>
> HEBREWS 11:6 (AMP)

People who believe in God, know, understand, and accept that God created the world with an intelligent design. They believe that it was God who created us—awesome and wonderful with such an intricately fashioned design that the greatest scientific minds have never been able to fully comprehend or reproduce.

> By faith we understand that the worlds [during the successive ages] were framed (fashioned, put in order, and equipped for their intended purpose) by the word of God, so that what we see was not made out of things which are visible.
>
> HEBREWS 11:3 (AMP)

When you acknowledge and fully recognize that God is The Creator of all, then you are in a position to accept the truth about your destiny. You must realize that God uniquely and masterfully created you and fashioned you for a great and mighty purpose.

> Have you not known? Have you not heard? The everlasting God, the LORD, The Creator of the ends of the earth, Neither

> faints nor is weary. His understanding is unsearchable.
>
> ISAIAH 40:28 (NKJV)

THE REVELATION OF YOUR PURPOSE IS PROGRESSIVE

Fundamentally, we see creation as a progression; it was developed incrementally. God could have created heaven and earth with all of its complexities in a moment in time. Yet we see God Himself progressively building His plan — day by day. Successful people who have identified their purpose did not fully understand it as a child; instead, it was revealed to them incrementally over time as they pursued it.

GOD IS NEVER IN A HURRY

God is strategic, focused, purposeful, deliberate, precise, and decisive, but never rushed. God holds eternity in the palm of His hand. He made time. He can take all the time He needs.

> But, beloved, do not forget this one thing, that with the Lord one day is as a thousand years, and a thousand years as one day.
>
> 2 PETER 3:8 (NKJV)

Don't be in a hurry to figure out your purpose. God would rather you take your time and get it right, than to miss His will for your life. This book is not designed for you to know your purpose quickly. It is created for you to understand the processes necessary to identify your God-given purpose.

This book lasts 10 days, whereas discovering, establishing, and maturing in your purpose takes a lifetime.

> Then God saw everything that He had made, and indeed it was very good. So the evening and the morning were the sixth day.
>
> GENESIS 1:31 (NKJV)

God saw *everything* He made and was exceedingly pleased; so much so that He did not change a thing — and that includes you. Behold it was very good!

EVERY MAN AND WOMAN HAS A DESTINY

You are a masterpiece, an original. Don't die a cheap copy! Be who God created you to be and live the good life! In Christ, it's never too late or too early, so seize the moment and soar with the eagles. Every man and woman has a mission from God to perform in this world, a mission for which their gifts and abilities precisely fit.

After discovering your mission or purpose in life, you should put all of the energy of your spirit, soul, and body into seeking its achievement. Whether you are called by God to manage a company, prescribe medicine, address juries, drive a forklift, work on an assembly line, sell products and services, serve as clergy, teach children, or manage a household, do it with all your might. It is your duty and your calling in life to fulfill your God-given purpose.

> And whatever you do, do it heartily, as to the Lord and not to men, knowing that from the Lord you will receive the reward of the inheritance; for you serve the Lord Christ.
>
> COLOSSIANS 3:23-24 (NKJV)

Now that you have an understanding that God made you with a purpose, you are ready to begin the journey.

1

DAY ONE

Discovering the Greatness Within

CONCLUSION POINTS

You have a specific God-given purpose, which was preordained before birth. God made man to have a relationship with Him and He expects him to spend time with Him. By seeking the face of God, you can receive revelation from Him about the purpose for which you were individually created.

When God formed the world and everything within it, He had a specific purpose in mind for all of His creation. From the stars to the seas, everything was designed to fulfill a certain mission, including the most precious creation of all — man. Just as the trees, the birds, and all the other awesome works of His hands have a particular function, you have a unique God-given purpose, and it is up to you to identify what it is. By doing so, you will not only please God, but you will also be empowered to live a full, satisfied, and complete life.

1

DAY ONE

Discovering the Greatness Within

KEY POINTS

- God has uniquely equipped each of us with innate abilities, gifts, and interests to enable us to fulfill our life purpose.
- You will never be completely satisfied or fulfilled until you are walking in God's plan for your life.
- God personally handcrafted you and placed certain gifts and abilities within you to fulfill a specific purpose in this life.
- Everything was created with a purpose and YOU are no exception.
- It is vitally important to your sense of worth and well-being to know and walk in God's perfect will for your life.
- Other people, including your spouse, children, family, co-workers, and friends will benefit from the awesome things God can do through you when you are operating in His divine plan for your life.
- No matter what decisions you have made in the past or how long it may take you to get into your purpose, the Lord will

redeem the time you have lost when you make a decision to operate in and fulfill your God-given destiny.

- The highest level of anointing and blessing is available to you when you are in God's perfect will for your life.
- It pleases God when you walk in the purpose for which He created you.

PRAYERFUL REFLECTION

Dear Heavenly Father, I thank You Lord and give You all the praise and glory. I pray that I will receive a revelation about what my purpose is; and I pray that as I write down my goals and complete the action plans and self-assessments on my 10-day journey to discovering my purpose that You will birth in me who I am and who You created me to be.

Lord, forgive me, as I also I forgive myself, for the mistakes that I have made in the past and I open up my heart to receive all that You have in store for me.

It is no accident that I am here; You fashioned me in Your very own image with a specific and great destiny. I have a purpose and You have uniquely equipped me with special abilities, gifts, and talents to fulfill an important and mighty purpose on earth.

Lord, I know that you are a progressive God and I pray that as I read this book each day that you will begin to reveal the things that You have placed on the inside of me. I pray that You will start slowly and reveal my purpose to me day by day, now and for the rest of my life that I may fulfill the calling You have placed upon me. Thank You gracious Father for making my life purpose known to me. In Jesus' name, I pray. Amen.

DAY 1: ACTION PLAN

Please use the *Prayers and Daily Journal* or the *Self-Assessment Workbook* as needed to complete the following items in your action plan.

1. Pray and thank God for creating you with a specific purpose.

2. Pray and ask God to reveal your specific purpose to you.

3. Whether you feel you are young or older, write down your life dreams in your *Prayers and Daily Journal.* (Ask God to reveal the dreams He placed inside of you.)

4. List 100 of your life goals in your *Prayers and Daily Journal.* Some examples include:
    - Receive a bachelor's degree in accounting
    - Own my own home decorating business
    - Purchase a four bedroom, two bath, ranch-style home
    - Secure investment properties, including apartment complexes and condominiums
    - Write a 200-page autobiography, chronicling my life
    - Travel to each continent
    - Amass a $1 million net worth
    - Have two children and raise them in the nurture and admonition of the Lord
    - Donate over $500,000 to my local church

- Meet and marry the woman of my dreams and love her as Christ loves the church

5. Think about this question: If all of your financial needs were met in abundance, what would you enjoy doing everyday, for the rest of your life without getting paid for it and be happy?

6. Scripture meditation: Psalm 139:1-17, Psalm 8:1-9

WORKPLACE
WISDOM

PURPOSE

DAY TWO

In Day 2, you will discover how your purpose is intricately and progressively revealed to you by God. Even as a young child, your interests, natural talents, and abilities reflected the greatness God placed on the inside of you before birth. You were elaborately and intricately fashioned in the image of God Almighty and He formed you with a magnificent destiny in mind.

2

DAY TWO

The Pathway to Discover Your Purpose – The Formative Years

When we think of purpose, we usually look at people who are in their purpose and are highly successful. One who quickly comes to mind is Bill Gates because he is the wealthiest American today according to *Forbes* magazine[2]. We often think of Bill Gates in terms of his industry leadership, riches, prominence, fame, and success. It seems clear that the man was created with a love for computer programming and we all recognize it is that love and passion which have taken him to fortune and fame, by God's grace.

PURPOSE REVEALED AND PURSUED BRINGS GREAT RESULTS

We are all familiar with Bill Gates. Let us take a closer look at his life because God has revealed insight, which can be gleaned from his life and others who have been extraordinarily successful in their purpose. Remember, the Bible tells us that the gifts and calling of God are without repentance. So, whether saved or unsaved, each person comes fully equipped with a host of inexhaustible gifts from God. However, it is God's plan and desire that every man come into the saving knowledge of Christ Jesus.

> For God so loved the world that He gave His only begotten Son, that whoever believes in Him should not perish but have everlasting life. JOHN 3:16 (NKJV)

William H. Gates, III, is chair and chief software architect of Microsoft Corporation, the worldwide leader in software, services, and internet technologies for personal and business computing. Microsoft had revenues of US $32.19 billion for the fiscal year ending June 2003, and employs more than 55,000 people in eighty-five countries and regions, according to Microsoft's web site.[3]

Born on Oct. 28, 1955, Gates, a Seattle native, grew up with two sisters and both parents. His parents encouraged their children to get involved in their (the parent's) lives. Bill worked as a page at the state capitol and in Washington, D.C., as his parents were involved in politics and business.

Gates attended public elementary school and took a keen interest in mathematics, business, and computing. At thirteen, he attended Lakeside, a private school where in the eighth grade at the age of thirteen, he discovered his interest in software programming. A schoolmate, Paul Gilbert, and his best friend, Paul Allen, both worked on computer hardware and programming. At school, they began Lakeside Programming Group (LPG) and learned everything there was to know about computers. The LPG evolved into a profitable business for the youths. During his years at Lakeside, Gates taught himself computer programming by understanding and improving upon BASIC, the language of GE's computer system.

In 1973, Gates entered Harvard University as a freshman, where he enrolled to study mathematics or law. "While at Harvard, Gates developed a version of the programming language BASIC for the first microcomputer, the MITS Altair."[4]

In his junior year, Gates left Harvard to devote his energies to Microsoft, a company he had begun in 1975 with his childhood friend Paul Allen. Gates dared to believe that the computer would be a valuable tool on every office desktop and in every home; they began developing software for personal computers and the rest is history.

Bill Gates discovered his purpose and life work at an early age. By the age of thirteen, he uncovered what evades most adults. He learned that purpose revealed and pursued brings great results. We're sure that Gates did not know that following his fire, passion, and gifting would result in his current status. But what about you?

You too have purpose on the inside. It is our goal to help you understand that and to encourage you to allow God to show you what yours is so that you can have a full and satisfied life.

PURPOSE IS REVEALED INSIDE OUT

Remember, God created you for a purpose. It is by getting in touch with what God put on the inside that purpose is known and revealed.

- It is something on the inside, which seeks and even craves external expression.
- It continues to knock at the birth canal awaiting its delivery.
- It is the quintessential expression of who we really are.
- It is the force that drives us beyond our greatest fears.

- It is the motivation that causes us to achieve the seemingly impossible.
- It is what causes us to transform the invisible into the material.
- It is what causes the mind to expand to heights of unparalleled creativity.
- It is what causes us to endure against all odds.
- It is what drives our capacity beyond our ability to produce.
- It is the essence of our existence.
- It is why we are here.

God has a path that is foreordained for you to follow. He has a specific pathway for you. This is called the *pathway to purpose.*

> You will show me the path of life; In Your presence is fullness of joy; At Your right hand are pleasures forevermore.
>
> PSALM 16:11 (NKJV)

HOW PURPOSE IS REVEALED

The revelation of purpose is incremental; it does not happen all at once. It occurs developmentally throughout one's lifetime. Let's begin with the formative years between the ages of two to seventeen. There are actions, steps, and processes that give insight into God's purpose for your life in the formative years. They include:

- Observation by parents or guardians
- Early childhood training
- Identification of motivational gift
- Education
- Hobbies and interests
- Exposure
- Character and morality
- Early job assignments

- Early mentoring
- Civic duties and volunteering

If you research and observe, you will notice that individuals who were either child prodigies or became great in the formative years did so by utilizing many of these factors to propel them into greatness.

Observation by Parents or Guardians

The perfect way for purpose to be revealed is found in the first institution formed by God — the family. In the beginning of the Bible, we see that God created a man and a woman and from that union came a child. Consequently, God's plan envisions that a husband and wife, mother and father, raise children together. Now, this may not be your case (for whatever reason), but it does not negate God's design. Do not check out here! God knew ahead of time what your situation would be — remember, He is omniscient (all-knowing).

Both parents are important because there are certain attributes that each gender brings to help develop the child. Beyond the primary care requirements, the parents are to observe the child with an eye toward determining their purpose.

> Even a child is known by his doings, whether his work be pure and whether it be right. PROVERBS 20:11 (KJV)

As with any great child, if you were to question the parents they would tell you that they noticed something in their child at a very early age. They might say, "I knew there was something about that boy that was different. He was always fascinated with color; it's no wonder that he enjoys his work as a top graphic artist." Or, "She always did like to talk. We knew she had a gift — talking everybody's head off at the dinner table reporting the events of the day with such detail. We know why she makes such a good newscaster. We always teased her and she got in trouble for it at school — now look at her."

OBSERVATION IS ESSENTIAL

Observation is a very powerful tool. Since communication is 93 percent nonverbal and 7 percent verbal, parents ought to pay attention to their children's personal expressions. Children are generally uninhibited at a young age when they are in their natural setting. Parents need to be alert for reoccurring themes in their children and observe continuity and repetitive behavior, which demonstrate patterns. A few key areas to pay particular attention include:

- Likes and Dislikes
    - What does the child like and gravitate to?
    - What does the child really dislike?

- Consistency of Interest
    - Pay attention to continuous themes of interest.
    - Notice what makes the child tick.

- Dreams and Desires
    - Listen to the child's dreams and desires.
    - Don't discount as rubbish what the child shares.

- God's Motivational Gift
    - Determine the child's motivational gift early.
    - Nurture the gift through your selection of educational, religious, and extracurricular activities.

The Pathway to Discover Your Purpose — The Formative Years

- How the Child Plays
    - Is the child physical?
    - Is the child investigative?
    - Is the child theatrical?
    - Is the child a reader?
    - Is the child athletically inclined?

- Social Interactions
    - How does the child interact with adults and other children?
    - Does the child enjoy being with people or being alone?

- Personality Disposition
    - Quiet
    - Social
    - Outgoing
    - Sense of Humor
    - Talkative

- Physical Attributes
    - Muscular
    - Strong
    - Fragile
    - Petite

- Mental Aptitude
    - Intellectual
    - Mechanical

- Notice the Differences between the Children
    - Do not force your children to be like someone else.

During the early stages of development, a child needs to be nurtured, loved, and affirmed. Early cultivation of gifts and talents is necessary. Appreciation and bonding needs to be evident in the relationships at home. A child must feel accepted and validated to blossom. Parents must go beyond the superficial and really pay attention to their children.

Early childhood training occurs from birth until the child enters grade school. It is a very important part of a child's development. God requires comprehensive development of children not only spiritually, but also in their individual gifting so that they may live a full and satisfied life and walk out their purpose.

Use your *Prayers and Daily Journal* to record your observations.

Godly Training Is Important

A child comes through their parents with an individual bent, which is given by God. A child's gift is always there — even if it is lying dormant. It's there!

> Train up a child in the way he should go [and in keeping with his individual gift or bent], and when he is old he will not depart from it. PROVERBS 22:6 (AMP)

Godly training of a child is important to help determine purpose, especially during the formative years. During the preschool years a child is growing exponentially and a parent must know the child, root and ground the child in God, and shape and mold the child into who God has made them. This requires much prayer and parental time.

In *Thinking for a Change*, by John Maxwell, we find the following:

> A survey was done to discover the creativity level of individuals at various ages. After all the testing, the statistics indicated

> that 2 percent of the men and women who were in their forties were highly creative. As they looked at younger people, the results emerged that 2 percent of the thirty-five-year-olds were highly creative; 2 percent of the thirty-year-olds were highly creative. This went on down to each age group until they reached the seven-year-old children. Ten percent of them were highly creative. However, further study showed that 90 percent of the five-year-olds were highly creative. Between the ages of five and seven, 80 percent of us who are highly creative develop an image, a picture, an attitude that we are not creative, and we begin to deny that particular part of our God-given equipment.[5]

God forbid that a parent shortchange their children.

Early childhood training helps prepare a child for their purpose. By developing proper etiquette, social graces, and common sense, a child can appropriately integrate into society. Lack of proper training can inhibit the full development of the child and eventually lead to a life of shame and ruin.

Importance of Identifying Your Child's Motivational Gift

An important step is to identify the child's motivational gift. There are seven motivational gifts, and they are outlined in Romans 12:6-8, which includes the perceiver, server, teacher, exhorter, giver, administrator, and compassion. This gifting is an individual's perspective or viewpoint of the world, and it greatly influences their attitudes, behaviors, social interactions, career choices, job satisfaction, and ultimately a person's purpose.

It is God's best that parents identify their child's motivational gift and nurture and support its development. God desires that you use discernment and not judgment; otherwise you may hinder your child's development. For example, a perceiver parent with a compassion child may tell him to toughen up if he expresses his sensitive nature. Yet God uniquely equipped him to be sensitive and perceptive to the emotional needs of others. If he is judged harshly for it, it may deter him from fulfilling his God-ordained destiny.

Thus, early identification of the motivational gift is critical. It aids and assists you in discovering your child's unique pathway to purpose. Days 5-8 address in detail how to identify the motivational gifts.

Formal Education

Once a child leaves home to begin school (unless home schooled) he begins to encounter a number of other influences that parents must maximize to achieve God's purpose in their child. It is the parent's job to use external resources to support God's plan and to defend against the external influences that attack and attempt to uproot and shake the child's foundation.

The purpose of education is to train a child spiritually, intellectually, socially, morally, and professionally in an effort to facilitate the identification and growth of the child's natural gifts, talents, and abilities. You can easily see that if a child enters the educational system before the parents have a clue about who the child is *from God's perspective* it would be easy for the child to get off track from the very beginning. This is why parental observation and training in the preschool years is so vastly critical.

Many parents leave the spiritual and natural educational growth and development of their child to the church or school system. Godly parents know that any educational system is a building block on top of what has already been instilled at home rather than an all-inclusive training ground.

Parents should evaluate whether the education is developmental, growth stimulating, and causing the child to blossom spiritually, academically, and socially. When a child enters the formal educational system, the parental observation skills should be on full alert.

The purpose of education is to provide basic skills which support purpose.

The beauty of education is that learning can take you places where you may never be able to go. It can teach you languages to communicate worldwide. It can teach you who you are in Christ Jesus and come into His saving knowledge. It can allow you to interface with people at all levels and differing walks of life. Education provides exposure. As education matures you and you grow in your gifts, it can bring you before great men. Education can also help you increase financially. Most importantly, education should facilitate advancement and further identification of the gifts and support life purpose.

> A gift is as a precious stone in the eyes of him that hath it: whithersoever it turneth, it prospereth.
>
> PROVERBS 17:8 (KJV)

> A man's gift makes room for him, And brings him before great men. PROVERBS 18:16 (NKJV)

The Educational System Should Assist in Identifying a Child's Gift

A comprehensive educational structure will allow the parent to observe and to know the rate at which the child learns, which skills are learned with a degree of ease, and which tend to be a struggle for the child. Some children are verbally gifted, while others are gifted mathematically or in the arts and theatre. Parents must know the areas in which the child excels and determine if that area is a part of their natural gifting; more than likely it is.

By the completion of middle school, parents need to determine if the child should pursue an academic or vocational curriculum, or both. These critical decisions should be made with much prayer and after close and long observation of the child's gifting and talents. The elementary and middle school years are defining. They represent the formalization of a life course direction. Great leaders and contributors to humanity and society are born during the elementary and middle school years.

Education usually takes place in groups or classes, yet it requires independent working conditions. Keen parents will learn if their child functions better in large or small groups, whether the child is more adept working independently or on a team, and whether the child exerts leadership abilities or prefers to play a subordinate role.

Parental Involvement Is Essential

The parent's involvement in the educational process is mandatory. The Word of God says people are destroyed for lack of knowledge. Generations have literally been destroyed due to the lack of knowledge on the part of parents concerning their children.

> My people are destroyed for lack of knowledge. Because you have rejected knowledge, I will also reject you from being priest for Me; Because you have forgotten the law of your God, I will also forget your children. HOSEA 4:6 (NKJV)

It is clear that if parents take a laissez-faire or hands-off attitude and abdicate the responsibility of developing their children, leaving it to an educational system, (even if a Christian school), there could be severe repercussions for both the child and the parent.

Noah Webster gives a godly definition of education in his 1828 Dictionary[6]:

> EDUCATION, n. The bringing up, as of a child, instruction; formation of manners. Education comprehends all that series of instruction and discipline, which is intended to enlighten the understanding, correct the temper, and form the manners

> and habits of youth, and fit them for usefulness in their future stations. To give children a good education in manners, arts and science, is important; to give them a religious education is indispensable; and an immense responsibility rests on parents and guardians who neglect these duties.

Hobbies and Interests

Hobbies present another opportunity for parental involvement to determine the purpose lodged within their children. It is an outlet to examine what the child likes and dislikes. What recreation does the child enjoy? Is it football, basketball, sewing, knitting, reading, or writing? What is it?

As a child I loved to journal, and it is no wonder that I have authored many books to date. It started when I was about eight years old. My husband loved science as a child. One Christmas, when he was a little boy, his parents gave him a chemistry set. His exploratory and systematic examination, observation, and testing continue to serve him today in several of our businesses, especially his orthodontic practice and his inventions.

Hobbies help define the innate interest of a child. It assists in bringing out what is genuinely on the inside of children and adults. Hobbies and interests provide insight into things the child is good at and aids in the identification of natural gifts and talents.

Interests awaken the inquisitive nature on the inside, aids in finding out what we are inclined to do, to like, and to be, and it is a good eliminator. It will rule out even for a child those activities in which they do not want to be involved.

Again, careful observation is necessary. We know two girls who love basketball. One wants to be drafted for the WNBA; the other loves to watch the game and playing has never crossed her mind. Both love the game of basketball, but only one of them is interested in playing it. This nuance makes a big difference.

We have a nephew who loves to tinker with cars and use his hands in almost anything mechanical. Furthermore, he does not like academics. He would do well in a trade school where he can excel and pursue his great love of fixing cars or mechanics.

Not every child is slated for college to achieve their God-given purpose, but every child must know their purpose to achieve their God-given destiny.

Here are a few factors to consider to help you determine a child's interests and hobbies:

- Does the child exhibit manual dexterity?
- Does the child enjoy sports and outdoor activities?
- Does the child enjoy animals?
- Does the child prefer to be indoors or outdoors?
- Does the child like to tinker with mechanical things?
- Does the child enjoy cooking or sewing?
- Does the child enjoy music and dance?
- Is the child a spectator or a participant?
- Does the child prefer group activities?

Use your *Prayers and Daily Journal* to record your observations.

Child Prodigies

Child prodigies are children who were observed, developed, steered into their gift, and matured into their purpose. We see them embracing and contributing their God-given gift to the world. People like Lord William Kelvin, Tiger Woods, Shirley Temple, and Wolfgang Mozart, to name a few throughout the generations, were all child prodigies.

Exposure

Early exposure to a variety of activities and experiences is another key to determining purpose. Exposure broadens horizons. As part of the developmental progression, it is critical that parents provide the proper godly exposure for their child. Further, it is important to eliminate exposure to ungodliness. Such influences as inappropriate television shows and negative media have had devastating effects on children. Ungodly video games do not challenge the mind, and many promote killing and violence as well as witchcraft and other demonic activity, which can shape the early developmental mind.

The performing arts, museums, libraries, church plays, and the theatre are great ways to expose children. It is widely known that children who attend camp away from home perform better when it is time to leave the nest than those who are homebodies. Overnight camp teaches a child how to receive instruction and direction in unfamiliar situations. It takes the child out of their familiar comfort zone and facilitates independence. It helps parents to identify areas where the child is not well adjusted and make the necessary modifications.

It is also advantageous to expose your child to your career. When a child can see what the requirements are for a given career, it gives him insight into what he needs to learn academically or technically.

Travel Is Important

Travel is one of the best and most comprehensive methods to expose a child to new experiences. Airplane, bus, and car travel all provide great means of exposure. God does not waste anything in the development of purpose. A parent may begin with travel outside of the immediate neighborhood, next travel within the state, then in the nation. Finally, travel around the world. If your family speaks English, travel to English-speaking countries first. If a child has studied a foreign language, venture out to a non-English-speaking country.

Learn to appreciate the difference in cultures, in foods, and most of all learn to appreciate other people. God loves people!

Travel exposes a child to a broader array of jobs and occupations than the child might normally see. Everything from street vendors, to ambassadors, entertainers, animal handlers, pilots, designers, models, and architects. This exposure is fundamental to purpose development.

Purpose May Be Hindered by Lack of Exposure

Purpose can easily be stunted if a child or their parents are afraid or unwilling to experience the unfamiliar. They must be open to travel, move, live in another country, or do whatever God has called them to do to fulfill their purpose. Just think, Joseph (Mary's husband) was obedient to the angel who warned him to go to Egypt because the life of Jesus was in danger. Jesus went to live in another nation for several years during His formative developmental years.

> ...an angel of the Lord appeared to Joseph in a dream, saying, "Arise, take the young Child and His mother, flee to Egypt, and stay there until I bring you word; for Herod will seek the young Child to destroy Him." When he arose, he took the young Child and His mother by night and departed for Egypt. MATTHEW 2:13-14 (NKJV)

Isaac left his homeland to go to Gerar in Egypt with his wife and the twins Esau and Jacob at the instruction of the Lord. Throughout the Bible, we see where parents like Isaac and Joseph (Jesus' parent) had to travel to protect their families, in order for their children to be in position to fulfill God's purpose in their lives.

> There was a famine in the land, besides the first famine that was in the days of Abraham. And Isaac went to Abimelech king of the Philistines, in Gerar. Then the LORD appeared to him and said: "Do not go down to Egypt; live in the land of

> which I shall tell you. Dwell in this land, and I will be with you and bless you; for to you and your descendants I give all these lands, and I will perform the oath which I swore to Abraham your father." GENESIS 26:1-3 (NKJV)

Parents today are called to do the same thing; namely to be available to God to go wherever is necessary to accomplish the divine destiny for their children. A godly parent must always follow the leading of the Lord. What a child is exposed to will help fulfill his purpose.

Character and Morality

The most important foundation for any child is spiritual and character development. Moral development helps to set a child on the path and keep him there. It is the parent's responsibility to instill the Word of God and godly character into the child.

As a child is developing, parents should be an extension of God in the child's life — teaching the child about God and taking the child to church with them where he can learn more about God. As the Holy Spirit draws him, of his own free will he can accept Jesus as his personal Savior and grow in the knowledge of God. Christian character development is most effective when parents live it daily, in the home and at work.

In addition to developing a love for God, a child must learn discipline, manners, and etiquette. Unless a child is disciplined, he will be rebellious, unmanageable, disrespectful, uncontrollable, and ultimately dysfunctional. This negatively influences his ability to find and fulfill his purpose. Listen to the Bible's warnings.

> Train up a child in the way he should go, And when he is old, he will not depart from it. PROVERBS 22:6 (NKJV)

> Foolishness is bound in the heart of a child; The rod of correction will drive it far from him.
>
> PROVERBS 22:15 (NKJV)

Clearly, parents have an enormous role to play in the godly development of the child that God has entrusted to their care. Churches often have programs to help parents facilitate the spiritual growth and development of children. Also, there are Christian organizations to aid in moral and character development.

Early Job Assignments in the Adolescent/Teenage Years (10-17)

During the adolescent years children are physically, emotionally, and academically maturing into young adulthood. Adolescents are generally going through a metamorphosis, but foundational building blocks have been set. At this stage, adolescents are seeking to establish their independence and identity.

Early job assignments are critical in developing and determining a child's purpose. Highly developed and successful people such as Bill Gates, Oprah Winfrey, Walt Disney, J.C. Penny, and John D. Rockefeller started working at the early age of thirteen or as young as eight. Adolescents learn at an early age those things they like and dislike. Parents are wise to expose pre-teens and teenagers to work experiences. We are not talking about household chores or sweat shops. Start by taking the preteen to your workplace. How will the child learn work ethics except through practical experience? The child will adopt the parent's perspective concerning work. Observation is a tremendously powerful tool.

Early job experiences are fundamental in helping a child identify their gifts, talents, and pathway to purpose. Early work experiences allow the child to determine what type of jobs and careers they enjoy and where their talents are best suited. For example, does the child like working with people, ideas and concepts, or with their hands? Is the child interested in a job as a corporate officer, secretary, manager, mechanic, doctor, lawyer, politician, firefighter, police officer, basketball player, singer, sales person, artist, or computer analyst? A youth's early desire to pursue a career may be placed there by God, parents, or society, and it must be discerned. A good indicator of God's plan is the youth's abilities to perform successfully and consistently in keeping with his desires and gifting. Many young boys and girls want to be professional basketball players but their abilities fall far short of the NBA or WNBA.

Early Job Exposure

Early job exposure allows a youngster to work in an environment and make sure their gifts and talents are in line with their desires. This can be accomplished through job shadowing and work experience. My husband often shares how he worked in his father's orthodontic practice at the age of ten and found that he loved working with his hands, in patient's mouths, and using his creativity to be of assistance in building others' self-esteem through orthodontia. Orthodontics allows him to use his hands and his mind to solve complex problems, and this is something that is very important to him. It is also what God has anointed him to do at a high level.

Conversely, he once told me of a time in his late teens when he worked in the auto factory. He worked there two years in a row and made substantial money. Yet, he said he knew he was never called to work in a factory after that experience; he knew that he was not anointed for that job. While he liked to use his hands, he was also highly academic. Because he is a teaching motivational gift, which will be discussed in Days 5-8, he needed an occupation that would allow him to also utilize his analytical ability. Therefore, when it came time to study for school, he studied hard to fulfill his purpose and he saved his money.

He later recounted his experiences as a Kirby vacuum cleaner sales representative. He knew he was not called to be in sales when he only sold two vacuums — one to his momma and the other to his grand momma. Consequently, for him to go into sales would have hindered him from fulfilling his God-given purpose and operating in the anointing the Lord placed on his life.

I graduated from high school at sixteen. It was the middle of the academic year, in December. I wanted to start college later that year in September when the normal college schedule began. Therefore, I found a job at Metropolitan Life Insurance Company on Madison Avenue as an actuarial data processing clerk. I knew then it was a means to an end—money for college. After taking that job, I was so motivated to go to college I took myself on my own college tour for a week.

Nothing is wrong with the jobs I've mentioned. They have proven to be awesome careers for others. There is, however, something wrong if working in a job facilitates a person being out of their purpose and thereby unfulfilled.

Early Work Experiences Are Important

Early work experiences help to rule out jobs and careers that are incompatible with gifting and talents. When a child spends his critical years watching television and playing video games, he is robbed of the opportunity to see what he does well; meanwhile, life is passing him by.

Early work experience is why some cultures develop higher than others do. Adolescents are exposed and get into their purpose at an earlier age and can maximize their contribution.

We were in Bangkok, Thailand earlier this year and observed children as young as four and five years old selling in their parents' businesses. This enabled them to learn skills, develop a life long trade, and generate an income stream — cash flow.

Without early job assignments, a young person could potentially spend years of time and money training for a career for which they are grossly dissatisfied. The average person works from ages twenty to sixty-five—that's forty-five years! God's best is that a person work until the end pouring out their gifts. It is very important to God that we spend our lives serving our purpose. The sooner we begin our life's work, the greater the contribution will be and the more powerful a legacy we establish.

Learning to Work under Authority

Another significant aspect of early job assignments is the opportunity for the adolescent to work under authority. Everyone has to report to someone. Whether it is a boss, a supervisor, a foreman, a board of directors, or to God Himself, we all have to learn to submit to authority. The inability to learn this skill can result in hitting a ceiling or being fired. This is a lesson best learned in adolescence.

Early Mentoring

While youth are experiencing the critical years of adolescent growth and maturation, it is imperative that mentoring takes place. Since youth are very impressionable at this stage, a parent must ensure that any mentor is a godly influence if they are to be actively involved in their child's life. Effective mentors can be instrumental in helping an adolescent determine his life purpose. Mentors along with parents can oversee the identification and development of skills and talents. Mentors can aid in narrowing down positions the youth is suited for and assist in procuring early jobs. They can help identify the youth's aptitude, skill level, areas of strengths and weaknesses, and provide helpful recommendations in line with the family goals.

Mentors can help steer a youth in the right direction. Mentors can fill in the gaps parents may have missed or areas in which parents are misinformed. They can assist in character development. Excellent mentors play a vital role in developing career and job readiness.

A godly mentor holds a youth accountable. Such accountability can help keep the youth involved in productive activities, out of trouble, and on a course directed to fulfill God's plan for his life. A mentor who is involved in the youth's life can counsel him through difficult times and teach him how to handle life's adversities.

Civic Duties and Volunteering

Once a child's foundation is established in the home, he begins to look outside the home for validation and affirmation of purpose. In school, a child can volunteer at an early age. As he grows and develops, he can build leadership skills, become a visionary, and further hone what he is good at. Most importantly, he can understand himself and further understand, sharpen, or locate his purpose.

When youth get involved in volunteering they can join groups, civic organizations or school clubs such as the one Bill Gates created at Lakeside to foster his interest in computer programming. Participation allows children to develop skills in effective social and leadership interactions, speaking ability, problem solving, and project management. It is not uncommon to find people who volunteered during their youth ahead in their development.

The Greater Good

Civic duty and volunteering is vital because it promotes an understanding of the greater good — life outside of oneself. People who want to contribute greatly to society, humanity, and the kingdom of God must get outside of themselves. When we look at great individuals who fulfilled their purpose, we see they poured themselves out to others. Mother Theresa, Dr. Martin Luther King, Jr., and Billy Graham are excellent examples. A young person can use the opportunity to serve as a method to establish what they want to contribute as a facilitation of their purpose.

Early childhood development, the adolescent years, and pre-adulthood are essential times of personal growth. Clearly there are a host of areas in which a parent and a child can grow and develop to be God's best.

2

DAY TWO

Pathway to Purpose – The Formative Years

CONCLUSION POINTS

Purpose is revealed incrementally by divine revelation from God. It is a powerful life force that inspires, motivates, and pushes you to achieve your absolute best.

From early childhood to adulthood, there are natural abilities that are evident in a child's interactions with others. Parents, and those in authority over children, are especially called by God to pay particular attention to their talents and gifting as they play a pivotal role in defining the child's life purpose.

From repetitive behaviors to interests, there are underlying characteristics that a parent/guardian/authority figure can look for that will aid in identifying a child's motivational gift and God-given purpose. Parents are charged with supporting the growth of their child's God-given gifting through:

- Observation
- Early childhood training
- Motivational gift
- Education

- Hobbies and interests
- Exposure
- Character and moral development
- Early job assignments
- Early mentoring
- Civic duties and volunteering

By selecting those educational and vocational systems that support the child's natural abilities and interests, a parent will not only aid in the maturation of their child's God-given talents, but they will also empower them to walk in God's best for their lives.

2

DAY TWO

Pathway to Purpose – The Formative Years

KEY POINTS

- Your purpose is revealed incrementally.

- Purpose is the essence of our existence, so it is critical that you identify it.

- When you are in the early stages of growth before external influences either aid or hinder the expression of your motivational gift, natural behaviors reflect your God-given gifting.

- Parents are called by God to observe and identify their child's motivational gift.

- God has charged parents with the responsibility of placing their children in educational, religious, social, and extracurricular activities that support the maturation and development of their God-given abilities.

PRAYERFUL REFLECTION FOR PARENTS

Lord, You have given me a powerful responsibility to identify and nurture the development and growth of my child(ren)'s God-given abilities. Lord, I accept this responsibility, and, according to James 1:5, I ask for wisdom in making decisions on behalf of my child(ren). May I only select those schools and activities that will support their God-given talents and abilities that they may grow and develop as You would have them. I thank You, Lord, for giving me insight to assist my child(ren) in growing and maturing in the gifts, talents, and abilities that You have endowed them with that they may fulfill their God-given destiny. In Jesus' name, I pray. Amen.

If any of you lacks wisdom, let him ask of God, who gives to all liberally and without reproach, and it will be given to him.

JAMES 1:5 (NKJV)

PRAYERFUL REFLECTION FOR ALL OTHERS

Lord, Your Word declares that You are no respecter of persons; and just as You knew Jeremiah before he was formed in the womb and called and appointed him to be a prophet to the nations, You also knew me before I was formed in my mother's womb and have called and appointed me to do great and mighty exploits on earth.

Because this calling was upon my life even as I was being fashioned, I realize that my natural behaviors as a youth reflected the motivational gift that You placed on the inside of me. Lord, I know that this gifting is to enable me to fulfill Your will for my life; and I pray now that by Your Spirit I will recall the innermost desires and passions of my youth. It is my prayer, Father, that You will bring back to my remembrance the goals, dreams, and desires that I had as a young child before life's experiences impacted my steps.

I thank You Lord that I will remember significant things from my past to enable me to operate in my purpose. May this new knowledge awaken a renewed sense of direction and meaning to my life as I take great steps toward gaining full revelation of my God-given purpose. In Jesus' name, I pray. Amen.

DAY 2: ACTION PLAN

Please use the *Prayers and Daily Journal* or the *Self-Assessment Workbook* as needed to complete the following items in your action plan.

For Parents or Guardians

1. Spend time before the Lord in prayer and ask Him to reveal things to you about your children that will enable you to help them determine their purpose. (John 16:13)

2. Begin to more carefully observe your child in natural environments, paying particular attention to his behaviors and

tendencies at a heightened level. Write down your observations in your *Prayers and Daily Journal.*

3. Write down your observations, including your child's habits, behaviors, thoughts, and so forth, in your *Prayers and Daily Journal.* Have your child journal as well.

4. Ask your child questions and observe his actions and behaviors to help you to narrow down his motivational gift.

5. Have your child share his innermost dreams and desires. Place them in your *Prayers and Daily Journal.* Have your child journal in his *Prayers and Daily Journal* as well.

6. Observe your child's hobbies and interests to gain insight into his natural abilities and talents.

7. Expose your child to a wide array of new experiences and occupations.

8. Demonstrate Christian character qualities and morality before your child.

9. Place your child in an educational environment that will promote his gifts, talents, and abilities.

10. Set aside time alone with your child to better understand his interests, thoughts, and goals.

11. Assist your child in finding job shadowing, internships, and part-time work in his areas of interest.

12. Assist your child in seeking excellent mentors.

13. Encourage your child to participate in civic and volunteer activities.

14. Be a person who understands and is committed to the greater good.

For All Others

1. Spend time in prayer and ask the Holy Spirit to reveal things from your childhood that will assist you in identifying your life purpose. (John 14:26) Make notes in your *Prayers and Daily Journal* of the revelations you receive.

2. Take time to reflect upon what you remember being interested in performing while growing up and write it down in your *Prayers and Daily Journal.*

3. Prayerfully think about what you enjoyed most as a child, what you were passionate about, and what excited you the most. Place this information in your *Prayers and Daily Journal.*

4. Write down your childhood dreams in your *Prayers and Daily Journal.*

5. Reflect upon early work, civic, and volunteer experiences. Think about the ones you enjoyed doing the most and write down what made those opportunities more memorable than others in your *Prayers and Daily Journal.* Note the areas you excelled in.

6. Ask your parents, siblings, other relatives, and close family friends about your behaviors and interests as a child. Write down their observations in your *Prayers and Daily Journal.*

7. Reflect on your education, training, and other experiences to identify your natural gifts and abilities and to determine whether you developed your gifts into talents.

8. As a child, which single occupation did you want to become more than any other and why did you choose it over others? Write that occupation in your *Prayers and Daily Journal* and prayerfully take it before God to see if it is His will for your life if you did not pursue it.

WORKPLACE
WISDOM

PURPOSE

DAY THREE

Day 3 focuses on the importance of determining your ruling passion and allowing it to govern your decisions on educational training, activities, and jobs that you undertake during young adulthood. God placed a ruling passion in you that reflects your innermost being. Uncovering your ruling passion is pivotal in discovering your God-given purpose.

3

DAY THREE

Narrowing Your Focus – Young Adulthood

Life work is a crucial stage in young adulthood. The pursuit of vocational or work purpose is one of the central anchors to keeping an individual on track and walking in the pathway of purpose. When young adults do not pursue life work, they tend to get involved in unproductive activities.

Throughout this chapter we will look at the lives of a few highly successful people who we would all agree operate or have operated in their purpose and dominated their life work.

JOHN DAVIDSON ROCKEFELLER, SR.

John D. Rockefeller, a devout Christian, was born on July 8, 1839 in Richford, New York. His father, William Avery Rockefeller, was a snake oil salesman, and his mother, Eliza Davison Rockefeller, was very religious and very disciplined. She taught John D. to work, to save, and to give to the church.

By the age of twelve, he had saved over fifty dollars from working for neighbors and raising turkeys for his mother. At the urging of his mother, he loaned a local farmer fifty dollars at 7 percent interest payable in one year. When the farmer paid him back with interest the next year, Rockefeller was impressed and later said: "The impression was gaining ground with me that it was a good thing to let the money be my servant and not make myself a slave to the money..."[7]

Rockefeller was able to perform difficult mental arithmetic and solve problems in his head — a gift that proved very valuable to him throughout his business career. In other subjects, Rockefeller was average. He never graduated from high school.

Rockefeller did not attend a four-year academic college but he did attend a ten-month vocational school at age sixteen where he learned bookkeeping, banking, and other business coursework. While his father was largely absent from his life, he did teach him how to construct notes and other business papers. Accounts reveal that his father believed in the importance of contracts. This was the formalization of the pursuit of John's life work. We say formalized because during his early childhood, Rockefeller was already developing into a successful businessman.

Rockefeller's First Job at Age Sixteen

At the age of sixteen, Rockefeller began looking for work in Cleveland as a bookkeeper/clerk. Business was bad at the time and Rockefeller had problems finding a job. Rockefeller visited every business in less than a week's time. He returned to many businesses three times. Finally, he got a job as an assistant bookkeeper with Hewitt & Tuttle, commission merchants and produce shippers.

Rockefeller impressed his employers with his single-mindedness, diligence, goodness, and honesty. He went to great lengths to collect outstanding accounts. He was pleasant, persistent, and patient and he successfully got the company's money from the delinquents. His low wage did not reflect his hard work. Nevertheless, he always gave money to his church as he was taught in his adolescence by his mother.

By age nineteen, Rockefeller's responsibilities had grown at Hewitt & Tuttle. He began to engage in trading ventures on his own account. He was described as naturally cautious and only undertook deals when he calculated their success. After he carefully weighed a course of action he acted quickly and boldly to see it to fruition. He was known to carry through very complicated deals without hesitation. The combination of being deliberate, precise, steadfast, and successful brought him attention and respect in the Cleveland business community. At this point, Rockefeller was developing his gift and participating in the society.

An Entrepreneur at Twenty

Several months before his twentieth birthday, Rockefeller went into business for himself, forming a partnership with a neighbor, Maurice Clark. Each man put up $2,000 ($36,000 in 1996 dollars) and formed Clark & Rockefeller — commission merchants in buying and selling produce. History records that after his first day at work, he went home, fell to his knees, and asked the Lord to bless his business. "At the end of the first year of business, they had grossed $450,000 making a profit of $4,400 in 1860 and a profit of $17,000 in 1861."[8]

Rockefeller was becoming a master in business and because he focused and developed his life work, other opportunities presented themselves for him to continue to excel, receive attention and respect, and increase financially. He never left God out and said that "God has blessed him with all of his money because God knew He could trust him to give it back."[9] He married at age twenty-five and had his first child eighteen months later.

Notice how Rockefeller's life work was developed and established. His focus or primary vocation was business. We can see purpose revealed in Rockefeller as a youth. Through parental observation and cultivation, his gifts were developed. As his life work evolved, we see further development in his pursuit of business education, which supported his natural gifting. He secured a job in his field and launched his formal life work.

We also see the influences of his relationship with God and his church, hobbies, civic duty, exposure in business and travel, character and morality, and early job assignments. He is a classic example of a young man getting into his purpose and pursuing his destiny.

YOUNG ADULT YEARS

During the young adult years psychological stakes are placed in the ground as you begin the pursuit of your life work. By eighteen, the formative and developmental years have laid the foundation for the future. Either vocational training, on-the-job training, higher education, or entrance into the job market is undertaken. The direction has been determined during the teenage years. This is an exciting time in life. It signals entrance into the real world. God's best at this stage is to see His children prospering and flourishing in their gifts and talents and pursuing open doors and opportunities.

Upon completing education and training, it is time to prove yourself in your purpose. All the practice, education, training, prayer, and relationships come to fruition as you step out into your first genuine assignment. We believe it is God's best for you to pursue one primary vocation, which will evolve into many opportunities. We see so many people trying to be a jack-of-all-trades and master of none. One primary vocation builds strength and depth while positioning for expertise and domination in your given discipline to the glory of God.

As a young adult every person confronts this question: What am I supposed to be doing with my life and am I doing it? Many are on the pathway to purpose, but others, due to a variety of reasons (discussed on Day 4), find themselves in young adulthood without a clue. Somewhere on the pathway to purpose, they were detoured.

We see so many people who delay or put off their pursuit and discovery of purpose until sometime in the future. Instead, they pursue external trappings, like money, prestige, and power, in hopes that it will lead to a satisfying and fulfilled life. Often, it does not.

Success can truly be found when you are operating in your purpose. Many people have a burning on the inside to pursue a particular path, but life and circumstances dissuade them. Meanwhile, they take up hobbies and volunteer activities that really express their ruling passion. Throughout life they say when I retire I'll devote my time to this or that. Sadly, they put off their passion for some mediocre pursuit, and often they never realize the greatness within. So, what does ruling passion have to do with purpose?

YOUR RULING PASSION

Your ruling passion is the ruling or governing desires and convictions in your heart. It is an intense, driving, and overwhelming sense. It is a deep-seated interest, which causes an energetic pursuit of an aim or devotion to a cause. You must learn your ruling passion and follow it.

Your ruling passion is the subject or cause for which you feel passionate. It causes your juices to flow. It excites you and commands your utmost attention. It might be a wrong you feel compelled to right or cause you feel everyone should stand up for. It can ignite your anger and stimulate your most important interest.

Your ruling passion is God-given and represents an important key to discovering your purpose and life work. Great men and women have identified their ruling passion and have developed their gifts and talents to make their purpose a reality.

What Awakens Your Ruling Passion

Your ruling passion is a concern or feeling that explodes on the inside of you. There are times when you can think of nothing else. It sometimes appears to be a driving force. For example, when you see someone else involved in the activity for which you are called or anointed to perform, something powerful and overwhelming is ignited within.

The ruling passion that the Lord has placed within you may become more intense during different stages of your life. However, this deep-seated, intense, burning passion is always within you, and it will be revealed throughout your life. Yet, it is usually revealed progressively as you transition through life cycles.

How Ruling Passion Can Be Revealed

Let me share an example from our own lives. My wife and I are called to develop television shows. The Lord began to deal with me about television, and every time I would turn on the TV, something would explode inside of me. Even though I had never thought about being on TV before, as I looked back on my childhood, I realized that several things were actually driving me in that direction. Yet, it wasn't until I was older that this passion started to explode on the inside, and I could think about almost nothing else.

Ungodliness is rampant on television and the Lord has placed it on our hearts to bring holiness back into TV programming. God desires holiness to abound in all walks of life, and He desires Christians to dominate to His glory in every walk of life — this includes television!

The passion was so intense that I would sometimes sit in church, and as my pastor would minister under the anointing, the Lord would begin to speak to me about television shows. Under God's anointing, an intense drive would come over me at a high level. It reflected an internal passion and it was something that God placed on the inside. I am sure about this because I had never before sat in church thinking about television, yet the thoughts would come unexpectedly.

Your Ruling Passion Hits at the Core of Your Being

When you observe someone else demonstrating or operating in your ruling passion, it ignites a fire within you. An overwhelming sense of fervor overcomes you as you observe them. This happened to my wife after the Lord began to speak to her about the two of us going into television.

One morning she was watching Joyce Meyers on television and heard her make a statement about being called to the world in the area of television. That statement hit at the core of my wife's being. When you observe your ruling passion in someone else's activities or work, it will strike at the very essence of your being.

Many things may excite us, but there are specific activities that we enjoy doing unlike anything else. So, when we see someone else performing those activities, it strikes us at our core. We observe them and begin to consider our own ability to perform that same task even better than they, or we desire to excel beyond their level of ability.

For example, if God has called you to become an artist and you walk into an art museum, all of the artwork will feel as though it is jumping right toward you. You will begin to think about your own ability and reflect on how you are able to do that just as well or even better than the individuals whose art you are viewing. Such thoughts reveal your ruling passion. These are uncontrollable thoughts that are ignited by the ruling passion God placed within you.

Your Ruling Passion and Your Career Choice

Your career decisions should be governed by your ruling passion. Selecting an occupation that you are passionate about enables you to excel at a high level. This is why identifying and operating in your ruling passion is so important. If you are not performing in your purpose and an obstacle comes against you, you may become deterred or sidetracked. However, if you are certain that you are operating within your purpose and an obstacle arises, you will remain undaunted and stand firm in your purpose.

Children Can Determine Their Ruling Passion

As children, many of our hobbies and interests reflect the ruling passion that God placed within us. Sometimes these interests are viewed as fads or youthful pleasures. They may be pivotal in helping us determine our life purpose. Our childhood activities and interests often reflect the God-inspired and God-given gifts within us.

It is critical to understand that your ruling passion is a gift from God. There are some who may know what their ruling passion is, yet they do not have a revelation that it was placed within them by God. Because of this, they may be discouraged or distracted from their pathway to purpose.

Do Not Be Dissuaded

You may feel that you are anointed as an artist and desire to become one. Yet if your family, friends, or others tell you that you shouldn't become an artist because you won't earn any money in that field, you may pursue another profession based on economic potential. If you do this, you will never realize your full potential nor will you feel satisfied or fulfilled. You were called and gifted by God for a particular purpose, and it is only when you operate in it that you find true satisfaction and fulfillment.

The opinions of others cannot be allowed to dictate your career decisions. Although those close to you may believe they have your best interest in mind, they may not be aware of your God-given purpose. Instead, your choices should be governed by the Word of God and His will for your life. However, you should remember that authorities placed in your life are anointed by God to help. Your ruling passion will be ignited when you are operating in His will.

Have the Courage to Follow Your Ruling Passion

My best friend and I attended the University of Michigan. He had always been musically inclined, playing in bands throughout high school, but he went to college to study medicine.

Because of his love of music, he decided to take his elective courses in the school of music. After taking a couple of music courses, he fell in love with the school and wanted to pursue a full-time study of music. But, his parents urged him to become a doctor. So he continued taking courses in both areas and struggled with what to do. He knew he had a burning passion to play music. He often told me that every time he would see someone singing or playing that he wanted to play behind them. Seeing others play music sparked something, because music was his ruling passion. He knew that if he became a doctor that he would only be doing it to please his parents. So after a period of time and taking courses in both areas, he decided to study music. His parents wisely supported him in it. Eventually, he married, and he and his wife formed a duet. Now, they perform all over the world and have been highly successful. They could not imagine doing anything else. It takes courage and honesty to pursue your passion.

Identifying Your Ruling Passion

Moreover, you can identify your ruling passion when you observe someone else operating in it and internally, you say things like, "I can do that better than they can," or, "I can do that too." There is an inner witness that confirms the thing you are gifted to do — something that you do with ease and confidence. There are innumerable possibilities. Your ruling passion could be:

- Art
- Ethical entrepreneurship
- Helping people eat better
- Meeting the needs of the poor and down trodden
- Improving the environment
- Music
- Preaching the gospel
- Photography
- Politics
- Protecting your country
- Raising children in a godly fashion
- Helping the sick to be healed
- Teaching people how to read and write
- Helping people relax and have fun
- Selling things to people
- Transporting people from one place to another
- Entertaining people
- Lifting someone's spirits
- Helping animals
- Saving the environment
- Making people laugh
- Saving lives

Success Results When You Operate in Your Ruling Passion

Highly successful individuals operate in their ruling passion. They function within a field or area that they are intensely passionate about.

One of our employees has an eighteen-year-old son who had many jobs as he tried to determine what he was called of God to do. The only thing he really loved to do was take pictures. Because of his love of photography, he built a dark room in their shed. Then, he would take pictures and stay in the dark room for hours on end.

One day, while speaking to his mother, we suggested that he should consider working in a camera store. Time passed and eventually he got a job in a camera store, selling cameras. He absolutely loved it. In fact, as soon as he walked in the camera store and started selling, he became the top salesperson. Why? Because he loved cameras. Someone who loves the product and has a passion for it is always going to sell more than someone who may be selling the product for income or another reason. The passion was within him, so he became much more successful in the camera and photo industry than many of his counterparts because that career ignited his ruling passion. So what is yours?

JOSEPH FRANCIS

Let's look at the life of Joseph Francis, the inventor of the lifeboat. At the age of twelve, Joseph was a page in the legislature of Massachusetts. Living in Boston, a coastal city, he learned of the unprecedented number of shipwrecks and life-threatening horror stories that occurred at sea. Even at his young age, he was deeply affected, which gave rise to his life passion.

He birthed the idea to create a life-saving boat. From the ages of twelve to eighteen, he dedicated his spare time to building and developing a life-saving boat prototype, fully equipped and tested to save lives.

After his dedication, diligence, and success, he submitted it to the Mechanics Institute in Boston. He had another idea from God to produce an iron vessel. He went to work and it took him six years to build the prototype. It is noteworthy to say that during these projects Francis's financial condition was dire. Therefore, he was not building out of his abundance or even sustenance, but out of his ruling passion.

One would think that his contribution would have been appreciated and explored, yet controversy surrounded it at all points. Rejected, he set out for the next two years to prove his invention worldwide. During his young adult years, he proved the success and was world acclaimed. He spent years in Europe building and manufacturing iron boats, vessels, and life-cars, floating docks, pontoon bridges, and wagons for five of the leading European governments.

Joseph Francis's name became great because of his commitment to allow his ruling passion to take root and give rise to one of the greatest life preservers — the lifeboat. Often, we allow money to limit our purpose. However, if we only trust the God-ideas that He has planted within us, we would have the answer to many of life's questions.

Just as Joseph Francis was angered and touched at his core when he heard about shipwrecks and lives lost at sea, you also may be angered and affected deeply by something. When you are angered by something, as Joseph Francis was, it can be the key to your purpose. It may be your ruling passion being demonstrated. So, rather than just getting upset about something, such as abortion or politics, you should examine your feelings and determine if your ruling passion has been awakened to do something or become something. This is why exposure is so important. If you are not exposed, your ruling passion may never be awakened.

DISCOVERING PURPOSE AS A YOUNG ADULT

Job Assignments

Entering the workforce is an exciting time during young adulthood. Job assignments should be carefully selected by identifying those that will train and provide a proving ground for your purpose. The best job will provide valuable skills, in-depth vocation tasks, and the development of people skills — all of which are important toward the successful advancement of your purpose. View mistakes and problems as opportunities for growth and development rather than as permanent setbacks.

Job shadowing is important at this stage because it will help you identify what area God has anointed you in and it will also reveal the areas that you will not excel in. For example, a young lady who desired to become an orthodontist volunteered in our orthodontic office. At the end of the summer, she realized that she was anointed in another area. Since that time, she has begun a successful marketing career. You can see why it is vitally important to select jobs based on your ruling passion, your deep-seated interest and your natural skills. Once you begin to do this, it will allow you to narrow down which job you have been called to perform.

Another example, if you can convince anybody to buy anything, you may know that you are called to be a salesperson. Yet, you may not know which products or services you should be selling. There are millions of things to sell, and you must narrow it down. Someone who sells clothing has a different anointing than someone who sells automobiles. Thus, it is important to first identify what you are skilled to do and then, begin to acquire different jobs that will allow you to hone in on the specific area of that career.

See your *Self-Assessment Workbook.*

Motivational Gift

During young adulthood, you should ideally have identified your motivational gift (see Days 5-8). You should also understand your strengths and weaknesses. You ought to know why you see life from the perspective you do. You should have begun to understand your purpose — how God designed and fashioned you. Self-acceptance should be high.

You should be motivated to employ techniques to temper your motivational gifts by identifying your weak points, and building into your repertoire of behaviors the attributes and actions that counterbalance your negative points. Now you are growing and beginning to realize your potential.

Specialized Vocational Development

In order to pursue your life work you may find yourself in a position like Rockefeller, who needed additional education. Specialized development may be educational training or it could be an apprenticeship. For example, to pursue a ruling passion in sculpture you may need to study the fine arts at a college that specializes in that area of interest. To help people medically, you may need to obtain a degree in medicine (MD) or registered nursing (RN) or licensed practical nursing (LPN), as well as state board licensing.

For some, on-the-job-training will prove to be the best teacher. Just get in the door and learn. We love what the ninety-five-year-old Rockefeller said to his grandson:

> Oh how blessed the young men are who have struggled for a foundation and a beginning in life. I shall never cease to be grateful for the three-and-one-half years of apprenticeship and the difficulties to be overcome, all along the way. [10]

The same sentiment was echoed about Joseph Francis.

> He crossed the Rubicon when his lifeboat was completed. The battle of his life was won by that early struggle. What manner of stuff he was made of was manifest then. The thought, tact, resolution, and force of character necessary to produce the lifeboat were competent to produce more and greater results.[11]

Focused Civic Duty and Volunteering

During young adulthood, you will want to be much more selective concerning the types of volunteer activities you engage in. Dedicate volunteer and civic duty time to activities you genuinely enjoy or those that will help you further develop your life work. Commitment to the church and church work is very important. Helping to build the kingdom of God is one of the most critical things that we can do with our time. Lending your skills to assist the church is pleasing to God.

If accounting is the area you have dedicated your life work to, lend your accounting skills to the church or a Christian organization. If you enjoy serving others, consider being an usher or helping in the church kitchen. Successful people are awesome volunteers. They are usually involved in civic and volunteer activities from their youth. Volunteering and involvement in civic activities in your formative years, will help you (such as in your school debate club, in the student council, or in your church) determine your strengths and weaknesses. By doing so, you will identify your skill sets. By putting yourself in different environments where your natural abilities, talents, and skills are needed, you can begin to tap into the God-given gifts within.

Volunteering also helps identify gifts, talents, and abilities. It also provides a platform for the development of a wide variety of skills including leadership, planning, administration, serving, public speaking, managing people, project management, and teamwork. In addition, it serves as an excellent place to find exceptional mentors.

Volunteering allows the individual to showcase and develop their skills in a relatively safe environment with minimal pressure to perform. It is an excellent place to develop important character qualities that are essential to success. These qualities include discipline, diligence, loyalty, endurance, respectfulness, and accountability. Seek to volunteer in your church first then other ministries. Once that has been satisfied, then volunteer in efforts that support the greater good of society.

Mentors

Mentors play a significant role in determining purpose. As a youngster, mentors play a more general role in directing the youth. However, as you mature, you should identify mentors who are successful in your life work and are willing to assist you. Seek godly men and women and pair with the same sex, men with men and women with women. In these times, it is important to also ascertain the Christian values of an individual before you get involved in any mentor situation. If you are married, seek the approval and support of your spouse concerning the mentor before initiating a relationship.

Excellent mentors serve as examples, help you grow, oversee your training, hold you accountable, and serve as counselors and support your development. Mentors will also help you identify your gifts, talents, and abilities and make sure they are matched with your goals and objectives. Excellent mentors are instrumental in helping the young adult discover their purpose.

Successful people have successful mentors. All of us can profit from the knowledge of someone else. This is why it is vitally important and beneficial to have a mentor that can aid you in your development.

When I completed my orthodontic studies, I went outside of our region to seek out a top orthodontic specialist to study under. Although I had never met him before, his outstanding industry reputation caused me to approach him. I told him that I wanted to learn from him so that I would be an excellent orthodontist. He talked to me, agreed, and began to advise me on what systems I should put into place and the advisors I should select. He opened his entire office to me. He taught me everything. Consequently, my office became one of the top orthodontic offices in our region within two years because of mentorship. I had the anointing of God to be an orthodontist, but if I had implemented the wrong systems or taken the wrong approach to operating my practice, not only would it have taken me a lot longer to become successful, it would also have been more difficult.

Therefore, as you are narrowing your focus and getting into your purpose, you must seek out individuals who are exceptionally gifted in that area and learn from them. This will empower you to become highly successful in less time and with more ease.

MARRIAGE AND PURPOSE IN YOUNG ADULTHOOD

Marriage is best suited for the individual who knows his life work and has undertaken it. Every individual has a God-ordained purpose that is governed by their motivational gift, ruling passion, and natural gifts and abilities.

When two individuals enter into a covenant of marriage, they become one flesh. Therefore, God expects the man and the woman to know and operate together in their God-given purpose. This enables them to have a harmonious relationship, because both individuals are operating in God's best for their lives. This is God's desire for a husband and wife. He desires them to support and encourage the maturation and fulfillment of their spouse's God-given purpose, which should ideally not be in conflict with their own. Such matters should have been sorted out prior to marriage.

In our case, we spent extensive time discussing our purpose and the assignments God had given us *prior* to marriage. We believed we heard from God as to the marriage; and during our courtship, we mapped out the plan of God to accomplish our God-given purpose and to have an exciting marriage. We have accomplished both, by God's grace.

> Therefore a man shall leave his father and mother and be joined to his wife, and they shall become one flesh.
>
> GENESIS 2:24 (NKJV)

Discovering Your Purpose after Marriage

What if you married before you discovered your life purpose? In spite of this, God has an awesome destiny for you and your spouse to fulfill. He has called you both to do great and mighty exploits on earth and He will anoint each spouse with the ability to assist in determining their life purpose.

God has a specific purpose for every man and woman to fulfill and has anointed and sanctified each marriage union to realize a great destiny on earth. Your life purpose, as husband and wife, should be supported by your spouse's life purpose. God has ordained a purpose for each of your lives, and He is depending on you to fulfill His will.

For a man, discovering and operating in life purpose is central because he is the head of the union. For a woman, it determines whether she can submit to the individual to whom God has brought her. After surrendering your life to Jesus Christ as Lord and Savior, marriage is the most important decision a person will ever make.

The Bible tells us not to be unequally yoked together with unbelievers. Anyone who does not have the same values, life objectives, and spiritual convictions is not equally yoked. If your spouse is unsaved and you are, the Word of God tells us the believing spouse sanctifies the marriage.

> For the unbelieving husband is sanctified by the wife, and the unbelieving wife is sanctified by the husband; otherwise your children would be unclean, but now they are holy.
>
> 1 CORINTHIANS 7:14 (NKJV)

Thank God that He has made it possible for our spouse to be covered. Further, it is wonderful to know that God created marriage to promote your purpose.

3

DAY THREE

Narrowing Your Focus – Young Adulthood

CONCLUSION POINTS

Once you reach young adulthood, you should ideally have determined your motivational gift and be in pursuit of your life work. This entails entering the workforce and pursuing a primary vocation that will evolve into many opportunities. Focusing your career on accomplishing your life work will help you remain single-minded and committed to fulfill God's purpose for your life.

It is critical that you pursue your life passion, which is your ruling or governing desire and conviction. It is God-given and represents a key to discovering your purpose and life work. Your ruling passion reflects the essence of your innermost being and should be used as a guide in deciding the vocational/educational training you may need, the civic activities you should become involved in, and the types of jobs you should undertake.

By pursuing your life passion, you allow yourself to discover your life purpose and begin to sit in the seat of your life work. Your life work is the work to which you dedicate yourself and achieve your greatest accomplishments. It reflects your God-given purpose, motivational gift, and natural gifts and talents.

3
DAY THREE
Narrowing Your Focus – Young Adulthood

KEY POINTS

- Ideally, by young adulthood, you should have determined your God-given motivational gift.
- A ruling passion is an intense, overwhelming, driving, heartfelt, deep-seated interest.
- Based upon your childhood interests, abilities, gifts, and talents, you should have identified your ruling passion.
- God placed a ruling passion on the inside of you, and identifying it is the key to discovering your purpose and life work.
- Your ruling passion should govern your choice of jobs, and more notably your life work.

- Life work is the work you dedicate your life to and the work that allows you to attain your greatest success.

- Civic duty, volunteer activities, mentors, hobbies, and interests should be selected based on your ruling passion.

- By beginning your life work, you will allow your natural, God-given gifting and abilities to flourish and develop, thereby increasing the likelihood of your success and prosperity.

- Undertaking your life work puts you in a position to receive a greater blessing from the Lord, enjoy a fuller and more satisfied life, and please God.

PRAYERFUL REFLECTION

Lord, I realize my most fervent and enthusiastic interests represent my ruling passion. I pray now that You will help me to identify it that I may begin to select the jobs and civic activities that will allow me to make my innermost dreams a reality.

I thank You now that as I identify my ruling passion I will begin to see the life work I have been anointed to complete. I know that once I start my life work and begin pursuing my ruling passion I will have immense satisfaction and an increased ability to achieve maximum results in my work. I thank You in advance, Lord, for this powerful awakening and revelation. I purpose to faithfully execute my life work as it is revealed to me. In Jesus' name, I pray. Amen.

DAY 3: ACTION PLAN

Please use the *Prayers and Daily Journal* or the *Self-Assessment Workbook* as needed to complete the following items in your action plan.

1. Pray and ask God to show you how to narrow and mature in your purpose. (James 1:5)

2. Perform the self-assessments for Day 3.
    a. Talents and Abilities
    b. Job Skills
    c. Work Environment
    d. Work Preferences

3. Identify your ruling passion and write it in your *Prayers and Daily Journal.*

4. Pray and ask God to help you identify your life work.

5. Select job assignments that match your talents, skills, and abilities.

6. Identify the type of volunteer activities that will help you further identify your life work and life purpose.

7. Identify and engage mentors who will help you determine your purpose.

8. Develop hobbies that give insight and will allow you to mature in your natural talents and abilities.

WORKPLACE
WISDOM

PURPOSE

DAY FOUR

Day 4 is the day of breakthrough! It reveals many of the obstacles that may arise along your pathway to purpose. There are countless reasons why you may get diverted, distracted, or thwarted from your pathway to purpose. Day 4 helps you locate yourself, make the necessary adjustments, and begin operating in your purpose.

4

DAY FOUR

Obstacles on the Pathway to Purpose

Jesus tells us in Matthew 7:13 that wide is the gate and broad is the way that leads to destruction, but narrow is the way which leads to life and there are few that find it. Often people refer to this scripture and say that the road is straight and narrow. However, the word *strait* refers to distress, strict, severe, difficult, or stressful. Jesus is alerting us and letting us know that we will be challenged as we pursue the life that He has preordained for us before the foundation of the world.

> Enter by the narrow gate; for wide is the gate and broad is the way that leads to destruction, and there are many who go in by it. Because narrow is the gate and difficult is the way which leads to life, and there are few who find it.
>
> MATTHEW 7:13-14 (NKJV)

We must find that narrow path. It is God's will for our lives. When we find it and walk the narrow path, we experience the life of which Jesus speaks. That life is *zoe,* the God-kind of life. How exciting to know that God wants us to live the God-kind of life here on earth and it is available to us as we walk out our purpose.

Jesus ends the statement by saying, "there are few that find it." How sad. Jesus forewarns us so that we might vigorously pursue and search out that narrow path and lead a full and satisfied life no matter what the enemy does to try to stop us.

Jesus tells us in this life we are going to have tribulations, but we are not to be ignorant of Satan's devices.

> These things I have spoken to you, that in Me you may have peace. In the world you will have tribulation; but be of good cheer, I have overcome the world.
>
> JOHN 16:33 (NKJV)

> Lest Satan should take advantage of us; for we are not ignorant of his devices.
>
> 2 CORINTHIANS 2:11 (NKJV)

To have victory, we must expose the work of the adversary and let the light of God shine, eradicating *whatever* the enemy has done to cause us not to live the God-kind of life here on earth. Let's allow the light of God to make us whole so that we can live the good life.

> If then your whole body is full of light, having no part dark, the whole body will be full of light, as when the bright shining of a lamp gives you light.
>
> LUKE 11:36 (NKJV)

STRAIT IS THE PATH

Recently we sat next to an attractive woman on a flight to Dallas. She was the picture of success. When she overheard our conversation on purpose, she jumped in. "Let me tell you, I am not sure that you can find your purpose. I've been in the legal field for the past seven years and I hate my job."

We said, "Inquiring minds want to know how you selected that career." She said, "It was my parents. They wanted a boy who would follow in the footsteps of my dad, but then I came along — a girl. My mom was unable to have children thereafter so they were stuck with me. Prior to his death, my dad was a corporate attorney for one of the Fortune 100 companies, and all of *this* was to please him. Law school was a struggle; I never had a passion for the law. I've often thought about quitting but my dad got me the job and the pay is good. What else can I do?"

We could clearly see her saddened heart. She felt trapped by her childhood rearing and the steering that forced her to become something she felt she was not created to be. She said on the inside there was a longing and heartache to be someone else, an interior design artist. She remembered that as a child she loved to draw and design home interiors. In spite of being called foolish and a daydreamer, the desire never left. "They can never kill my real passion," she said. Her parents probably did the best they could in hopes of equipping their only child for a successful life. Oftentimes, parents impose their goals and dreams on their children.

As the plane was landing, almost tearfully she said, "I guess I've got to make a decision because I don't know how long I can go on being unhappy." We prayed for her and asked the Lord to give her wisdom and to direct her path. She gave her life to the Lord that day and left with renewed hope.

We have also seen situations in which parents have had little to no involvement in developing their children. Well-meaning parents may say things like, "Get a good job," "Get a good education," or, "Make something of yourself." But vague directives are not constructive in the developmental process.

Conversely, we have seen parents who have understood their children and supported them by not imposing their unfulfilled desires on their children; instead they embraced who God made their children to be.

YOU WERE BORN WITH A GREAT PURPOSE

You are born with your purpose already intact. God could not have made it any simpler. Yet unknowing parents, other individuals, or you, can wreak havoc in the developmental process of life. This is not a finger pointing session. Our adversary is the deceiver who uses people to try to destroy the work of God.

> Be sober, be vigilant; because your adversary the devil walks about like a roaring lion, seeking whom he may devour.
>
> 1 PETER 5:8 (NKJV)

The Bible tells us who our real battle is against.

> For we do not wrestle against flesh and blood, but against principalities, against powers, against the rulers of the darkness of this age, against spiritual hosts of wickedness in the heavenly places. EPHESIANS 6:12 (NKJV)

Even in the best cases, we have seen individuals get off track in some area of their lives because they were undeveloped in a particular aspect of their purpose. In this chapter we will explore the sources of derailment and how to get back on track.

We must understand that every great person has overcome major obstacles on their path to fulfill their purpose. Such problems are not unique. So realize that problems may arise along your pathway to purpose. Prepare yourself, gird yourself up, and know that you can do all things through Jesus Christ.

> I can do all things through Christ who strengthens me.
>
> PHILIPPIANS 4:13 (NKJV)

In the remainder of this chapter, let us look at a few of the most common obstacles that hinder people from getting on and staying on the pathway to purpose.

UNSTABLE FAMILY RELATIONSHIPS

Divorce causes emotional and economic instability. It often diverts attention to dealing with pain of the past and finding ways to rebuild your life. Family upheaval can impair development for all family members. Look at these statistics from the United States Bureau of Statistics, reprinted by the Divorce Center[12].

- In 1998, 2.2 million couples married and 1.1 million couples divorced.
- In 2000, 58 million couples were married, yet separated.
- In 2000, there were over 21 million divorces.
- People between the ages of twenty-five to thirty-nine make up 60 percent of all divorces.
- Over 1 million children are affected by divorce each year.
- Approximately one third of divorced parents remain bitter and hostile several years after the divorce.

See your *Self-Assessment Workbook*.

Incest and Sexual Abuse

Sexual abuse is widespread in this nation. Statistics indicate that 80 percent of sexual abuse takes place before the age of 30. Alarmingly, 61 percent takes place prior to the age of 18 and the person who committed the act is usually known by the victim as a family member, close relative, or a person in authority over the child.

- Research indicates that 46 percent of children who are raped are victims of family members.[13]

- The majority of American rape victims (61 percent) are raped before the age of 18; furthermore, an astounding 29 percent of all forcible rapes occurred when the victim was less than 11 years old. Eleven percent of rape victims are raped by their fathers or stepfathers, and another 16 percent are raped by other relatives.[14]

- In a study of male survivors of child sexual abuse, over 80 percent had a history of substance abuse, 50 percent had suicidal thoughts, 23 percent attempted suicide, and almost 70 percent received psychological treatment. Thirty-one percent had violently victimized others.[15]

According to a 1999 report from the Federal Bureau of Investigations:[16]

- one in four girls will be sexually assaulted by the time they are eighteen years old.
- one in six boys will be sexually assaulted by the time they are eighteen years old.
- one in three women will be raped in her lifetime.
- one in five men will be sexually assaulted in his lifetime.

And according to a 2001 report from the Center Against Sexual Abuse (CASA), reprinted by the Southeast Missouri Network Against Sexual Violence:[17]

- It is estimated that 10 percent of all sexual assaults happen to men.
- Only 16 percent of all rapes are reported to the police.
- 46 percent of rape survivors consider or attempt suicide.

These are examples of the works of the adversary against the plan of God. Nevertheless, the devil is a liar and the father of lies and we are able to overcome him by the blood of the Lamb.

> And they overcame him by the blood of the Lamb and by the word of their testimony, and they did not love their lives to the death. REVELATION 12:11 (NKJV)

One Parent, Premature Death of a Parent, or Orphan

Whether due to death, divorce, an absent spouse, or unmarried parents, children who do not have two parents miss out during the critical formative years. Their development can be negatively affected with feelings of being unloved, abandoned, or empty. Unless identified and dealt with at an early age, such a person has a greater likelihood of experiencing maladjustment and low self-esteem that can cause them to get off the pathway to purpose.

Controlling and Manipulative Parents

Some parents are very controlling and manipulative, which has a tendency to either break the spirit of a child or cause a child to become rebellious. In either case, such parental behavior does not support the child's development into their life purpose.

Possible Problems

Here are some problems that you could have experienced as a result of unstable family relationships:

- Parents steering their children in the wrong direction
- Family members and extended family involved in varying types of abuse against children
- Involvement in abusing others
- Financial stress due to single parenting
- Foster care or adoption
- Forced into an incompatible career pathway
- Coerced into activities by domineering parents
- Experienced feelings of emptiness and felt unloved

Action Steps

If you have experienced any of these problems, do not despair. Let us look at some steps you can take to help you get back on track.

- If you are not a believer in the Lord Jesus Christ, give your life to the Lord. Only through His power can you be freed of these bondages and fully enjoy your pathway to purpose as God has planned it.

- Forgive any family member or any other person who knowingly or unknowingly hurt you. (This may include you.) Truly forgive as Christ forgave you. Find a way to be a blessing to them, where appropriate. The greatest gift may be just forgiving them or yourself.

> For if you forgive men their trespasses, your heavenly Father will also forgive you. But if you do not forgive men their trespasses, neither will your Father forgive your trespasses.
>
> MATTHEW 6:14-15 (NKJV)

> Therefore if you bring your gift to the altar, and there remember that your brother has something against you, leave your gift there before the altar, and go your way. First be reconciled to your brother, and then come and offer your gift.
>
> MATTHEW 5:23-24 (NKJV)

> And whenever you stand praying, if you have anything against anyone, forgive him, that your Father in heaven may also forgive you your trespasses. But if you do not forgive, neither will your Father in heaven forgive your trespasses.
>
> MARK 11:25-26 (NKJV)

- Pray and ask God to help remove any bitterness in your heart toward them. Seek Christian counseling through your church or a counseling service referred by your church, if necessary.

> Let all bitterness, wrath, anger, clamor, and evil speaking be put away from you, with all malice. EPHESIANS 4:31 (NKJV)

- Do not allow yourself to compensate for this void with ungodly relationships or behaviors.

- Pray and ask God to show you how to fill the void through a deeper relationship with the Lord.

- Join and get involved in a strong local Christian church that teaches the Bible. Look for a church that is full of love. Become an active part in the family of believers, the body of Christ.

- Develop godly relationships with mature Christians to fill the void. Don't develop relationships with the opposite sex.

Women should seek older mothers or deaconesses and men should seek deacons or senior elders in the church.

- Find others who have similar pains, hurts, and voids and allow God to use you to help them resolve their pain as you grow and mature in the things of God. This takes the focus off of yourself. Be a giver.

AUTHORITIES DID NOT HELP YOU DEVELOP YOUR TALENTS

Parents and Extended Family

Parents and family are a gift from God. Most do the best they can, but they are not perfect. Depending on their background, education, age, emotional stability, financial wherewithal, exposure, mentors, success, education, and commitment to Christ, their input will vary in what they can give.

Parents who do not understand that God created children with a life purpose may not be in their own life purpose. Thus, they won't be training their children to understand this. Parents' lives may be filled with frustration and difficulties, so they just do not have it to give. Therefore, a child can suffer throughout childhood and into their adult life.

Disinterested Teachers and Counselors

Even the most balanced teachers and counselors can be biased. People who are biased will give more attention to some than others based on their own prejudices. This can influence a child's pathway to purpose. Low achievement and low expectations are sometimes imposed on children because some of their teachers or counselors hate their jobs and are just in it for a paycheck — they are out of their purpose.

See your *Self-Assessment Workbook.*

Supervisors and Bosses

Work conditions can be such that employees' skills, talents, and development are minimized while the needs of the organization are maximized. Often training and growth are geared toward the success of the organization and not the individual. Unless the individual goes into the job market knowing their purpose or at least having a clear path laid out, it is unlikely that the workplace authorities will reinforce and encourage individual growth — especially if it is not compatible with the organization.

Poor Mentors

Poor mentors do not take the time to work with their advisees, so growth is stifled, accountability is lacking, identifying life purpose suffers, and professional development is not accelerated.

On occasion, mentor and advisee relationships have evolved into ungodly pursuits, for that reason an individual must pray and have an excellent referral prior to submitting to the leadership of a mentor.

Possible Problems

Here are some problems that you could have experienced at the hands of authorities:

- You were asked or made to be someone whom you are not called to be
- You were intentionally misguided
- You were told you could not or would not amount to anything

- Your God-given gifts and talents were ignored and not recognized
- You were overlooked or discriminated against
- No one took a serious interest in your personal, spiritual, academic, or social development
- Mentors, teachers, parents, or bosses took advantage of you

Action Steps

- If you are not a believer in the Lord Jesus Christ, give your life to the Lord because it is only through His power that you can be freed of these bondages and fully enjoy your pathway to purpose as God has planned it.

- Forgive those authorities who have not, did not, or will not help you.

- Study God's Word and find out who you are in Christ Jesus.

> And you are complete in Him, who is the head of all principality and power. COLOSSIANS 2:10 (NKJV)

> Looking unto Jesus, the author and finisher of our faith, who for the joy that was set before Him endured the cross, despising the shame, and has sat down at the right hand of the throne of God. For consider Him who endured such hostility from sinners against Himself, lest you become weary and discouraged in your souls.
>
> HEBREWS 12:2-3 (NKJV)

- Seek God's direction to know where you should be at this juncture in your life and who should help you get there.

> For I know the thoughts that I think toward you, says the LORD, thoughts of peace and not of evil, to give you a future and a hope. JEREMIAH 29:11 (NKJV)

> Call to Me, and I will answer you, and show you great and mighty things, which you do not know.
> JEREMIAH 33:3 (NKJV)

- Pray and ask God to bring godly mentors who can help you identify and develop your God-given abilities.

- Seek out godly mentors including your pastor, mature Christians, and other Christian professionals who are knowledgeable in your field and willing to help you.

- We strongly urge godly same sex mentors. They should be of the same marital status and you should have full disclosure and agreement with your spouse.

- Avoid ungodly mentors — they can cause the anointing on your life to be lifted while taking the focus off of godly pursuits.

WRONG RELATIONSHIPS

Ungodly Relationships

This area is probably among the most critical in its impact, resulting in people getting out of their purpose. God made us and He loves people. It is His desire to positively influence people by His Word, the Bible. Yet today's society is fraught with people who are doing whatever it takes to make it happen — even if it means compromise and breaking the law.

Social relationships and business relationships have a bearing on what happens in your life. Ungodly relationships do not just mean gangs. They include improper and destructive romantic relationships, unproductive friendships, and inappropriate work relationships. Gangs are designed to replace the family. The children who join gangs are seeking acceptance and approval. They will commit crimes and even take another's possessions and precious life to be accepted. The consequences of gang life are similar to white collar crime and the old boy network. Let's take a closer look at some different ungodly relationships.

- Gang relationships usually involve:
  - Destructive and abusive behavior
  - Illegal activity
  - Violence and anger-driven behavior
  - Malignment
  - Criminal record and jail time
  - Skewed view of life
  - Rebellion and disrespect for established authority

- Destructive romantic relationships can result in:
  - Poor self-image
  - Low self-esteem
  - Physical and verbal abuse
  - Depression and suicide

- Unproductive friendships are:
  - Time wasters
  - Distractions
  - Stressful and demanding
  - Robbers of personal growth and development

- Inappropriate work relationships can cause:
    - Breeches of character and integrity
    - Laziness and slothfulness
    - Lack of respect and appreciation for authority
    - Focusing on getting money rather than developing your gifts and talents

- Wrong friendships often:
    - Take you off focus
    - Produce ungodly behaviors
    - Pull you down when you are trying to succeed

See your *Self-Assessment Workbook.*

Possible Problems

Wrong relationships can result in a host of problems. These are some you may have experienced:

- Ungodly and immoral activities
- Prevention from being God's best
- Open discouragement
- Being pulled down
- Unhealthy competition among friends
- Inappropriate romantic involvements for advancement
- Premature death of a loved one
- Jail time and a criminal record
- Emotional instability
- Decline in productivity
- White collar criminal activity
- Adulterous and immoral relationships
- Frustration and anxiety

Action Steps

- Pray and seek the Lord concerning who you are to be in association with at work and socially, including all friendships.

- Study the Bible and pray the Word of God to protect you from ungodly relationships.

  You shall keep them, O LORD, you shall preserve them from this generation forever. PSALM 12:7 (NKJV)

  The LORD will preserve him and keep him alive, And he will be blessed on the earth; You will not deliver him to the will of his enemies. PSALM 41:2 (NKJV)

  "Because he has set his love upon Me, therefore I will deliver him; I will set him on high, because he has known My name." PSALM 91:14 (NKJV)

- Study the Scripture and know God's heart concerning ungodly associations. (Psalm 1, 5:9, and 101:7; Proverbs 7:10, 14:8, 20:14-15, 20:18, 20:22, 20:23)

- Immediately remove yourself from the ungodly relationship or situation. You can ask God for strength, but God gives us freewill and it is your responsibility to correct the situation. It is a decision.

- Seek godly friendships and relationships. Look in your church. Become involved in church groups and organizations that have a Christian focus. No matter what your station in life you should serve and fellowship in the body of Christ.

- Know that God loves you and He would never encourage you to be in a destructive, debasing, and shameful relationship or situation.

SUBSTANCE ABUSE AND DESTRUCTIVE HABITS

Drug Use and Alcohol

Research has documented that children with substance-abusing parents are more at risk than their peers for alcohol and drug use, delinquency, depression, as well as poor school performance.

Results indicate that a larger percentage of very young children are more likely than older children to live in a household where one or both parents use illicit drugs. This is most likely driven by the fact that younger parents are more likely than older parents to use illicit drugs, and such parents also tend to have younger children.

Based on the Substance Abuse and Mental Health Services Administration's (SAMHSA), National Household Survey, in 2001 more than 6 million children lived with at least one parent who abused or was dependent on alcohol or an illicit drug during the past year. This involved about 10 percent of children aged five or younger, 8 percent of children aged six to eleven, and 9 percent of youths aged twelve to seventeen.[18]

Prescription and illegal drugs, alcohol, and cigarette abuse are not only harmful to the user but also to the next generation.

Compulsive Shopping and Overspending

It is well known that personal debt is crippling many American families. According to www.neway.org/debtStatistics.html:

- The average balance on a credit card is $8,000.
- The average interest rate is 18.9 percent.
- Late fees now average $29-$35.

- The average household has ten credit cards.

- If your credit card balance is (the average) $8,000, and you make the minimum monthly payment at 18.9 percent (the average) interest, it will take you twenty-five years and seven months to pay the debt off. You will pay $15,432 in interest charges, bringing your total paid to $23,432!

- Americans paid out approximately $65 billion in interest last year alone.

- Credit card companies solicit the average American seven times a year through the mail.

- The typical minimum monthly payment is 90 percent interest and 10 percent principal.

Aside from running up credit card debt, other problem spending includes compulsive shopping, gambling, and playing the lottery.

Unless your spending is under control, your finances can take you off your course and life purpose.

Possible Problems

Possible problems and consequences caused by substance abuse and destructive habits include:

- Lowered resistance to immorality
- Permanently damaged and impaired brain and thought processes
- Seriously impaired health
- Weight gain and medical impairments
- Financial bankruptcy
- Death

Action Steps

- Pray and ask God for deliverance.

- Get into a very good Christian drug abuse program.

  And do not be drunk with wine, in which is dissipation; but be filled with the Spirit. EPHESIANS 5:18 (NKJV)

  Wine is a mocker, strong drink is a brawler, and whoever is led astray by it is not wise. PROVERBS 20:1 (NKJV)

- Cut up the credit cards.

  A faithful man will abound with blessings, But he who hastens to be rich will not go unpunished.
  PROVERBS 28:20 (NKJV)

- Take the *Dominating Money* course offered by the Eagans through www.workplacewisdominstitute.com.

  Now godliness with contentment is great gain.
  1 TIMOTHY 6:6 (NKJV)

  And He said to them, Guard yourselves and keep free from all covetousness (the immoderate desire for wealth, the greedy longing to have more); for a man's life does not consist in and is not derived from possessing overflowing abundance or that which is over and above his needs. LUKE 12:15 (AMP)

- Fill yourself so full of God's Word that you have room for nothing else.

- Remove yourself from all destructive relationships, behaviors, and activities and replace them with godly ones.

> Do not be unequally yoked with unbelievers [do not make mismated alliances with them or come under a different yoke with them, inconsistent with your faith]. For what partnership have right living and right standing with God with iniquity and lawlessness? Or how can light have fellowship with darkness? 2 CORINTHIANS 6:14 (AMP)

> Therefore submit yourselves to every ordinance of man for the Lord's sake, whether to the king as supreme, or to governors, as to those who are sent by him for the punishment of evildoers and for the praise of those who do good.
> I PETER 2:13-14 (NKJV)

- Leave the past in the past — move on!

> Brethren, I do not count myself to have apprehended; but one thing I do, forgetting those things which are behind and reaching forward to those things which are ahead, I press toward the goal for the prize of the upward call of God in Christ Jesus. Therefore let us, as many as are mature, have this mind; and if in anything you think otherwise, God will reveal even this to you. PHILIPPIANS 3:13-15 (NKJV)

- Study scriptures dealing with the areas you need to concentrate on.

LACK OF GODLY CHARACTER

Consider these ungodly attitudes and behaviors: immorality; laziness;

a guilty conscience ; rebellion; lack of discipline; procrastination; pride and arrogance; emotional instability; envy; lack of creativity; greed; fear; lack of sound, moral ethics; and integrity.

One of the greatest causes of derailment in the area of unfulfilled purpose is a lack of strong sustainable character. Lack of discipline is a time waster, and time is our most valuable commodity. Oftentimes people are lazy and unwilling to apply the gifts and abilities that God has so richly given. They are not unwilling because of a handicap, disfigurement, or physical inability but simply because of procrastination, laziness, and lack of discipline. But, opportunity waits for no one.

An ungodly focus will support all negative attitudes and behaviors and cause difficulty, hurt, and loss. The examples of the WorldCom, Enron, and Arthur Andersen scandals are a direct reflection of a lack of integrity and greed.

Another culprit of character default is busyness. Many people today say that they are so busy; but the question is busy doing what. Busyness that is not focused on life purpose is dangerous, wastes time, and disrupts the effective development of the individual.

See your *Self-Assessment Workbook.*

Possible Problems

Ungodly character can result in numerous problems and consequences such as these:

- Lack of focus
- No energy to fuel the vision
- No initiative or creativity
- Unreliable, resulting in lost opportunities
- Not able to get along with people
- Insecure and untrusting
- Negative, competitive, and backbiting

- Lack of values for a successful life
- Willing to lie, steal, and cheat to make money
- Willing to destroy self and others

See your *Self-Assessment Workbook.*

Action Steps

- Repent before God for having ungodly behavior.

  If we confess our sins, He is faithful and just to forgive us our sins and to cleanse us from all unrighteousness.

  1 JOHN 1:9 (NKJV)

- Purpose to develop godly behaviors and always remember that exercising good character is a learned behavior.

- Read the Bible and study scriptures on godly character.

- Read a chapter from the Book of Proverbs each day for a year.

- Study the lives of people who have developed strong positive character and glean wisdom from them.

- Know that no matter what you have done, God loves you and He wants you to walk upright before Him so that you can be a mighty demonstration of Him on earth. You are His ambassador on earth.

  Now then, we are ambassadors for Christ, as though God were pleading through us: we implore you on Christ's behalf, be reconciled to God. 2 CORINTHIANS 5:20 (NKJV)

RELIGIOUS TOLERANCE

An Open Door

Dabbling or participating in other religions can open the door to Satan. There are numerous other religions and you may think some of them are harmless, but they are not. Examine this list: witchcraft; astrology; occult; wiccans — demonology; voodoo; satanism; cults; obiah; fortune tellers, palm readers, tea leaf readers; ouji boards, Harry Potter and witchcraft spells; tarot cards; and spiritual "readers."

All of these are harmful. They try to serve as the moral and ethical guide to issues and problems. But, God's Word must be our guide.

Problems and Consequences

Participation in these activities will likely result in:

- Defiance against God
- Demonic possession
- Demonic oppression

> There shall not be found among you anyone who makes his son or his daughter pass through the fire, or one who practices witchcraft, or a soothsayer, or one who interprets omens, or a sorcerer, or one who conjures spells, or a medium, or a spiritist, or one who calls up the dead. For all who do these things are an abomination to the LORD, and because of these abominations the LORD your God drives them out from before you. You shall be blameless before the LORD your God.
>
> DEUTERONOMY 18:10-13 (NKJV)

> You shall not eat anything with the blood, nor shall you practice divination or soothsaying. LEVITICUS 19:26 (NKJV)

> Give no regard to mediums and familiar spirits; do not seek after them, to be defiled by them: I am the LORD your God.
>
> LEVITICUS 19:31 (NKJV)

> And the person who turns to mediums and familiar spirits, to prostitute himself with them, I will set My face against that person and cut him off from his people.
>
> LEVITICUS 20:6 (NKJV)

> Now the works of the flesh are evident, which are: adultery, fornication, uncleanness, lewdness, idolatry, sorcery, hatred, contentions, jealousies, outbursts of wrath, selfish ambitions, dissensions, heresies, envy, murders, drunkenness, revelries, and the like; of which I tell you beforehand, just as I also told you in time past, that those who practice such things will not inherit the kingdom of God.
>
> GALATIANS 5:19-21 (NKJV)

These false religions may serve as the pathway to devil worship. They also cause you to trust in people and in ungodly doctrine that goes against God's Word.

> All Scripture is given by inspiration of God, and is profitable for doctrine, for reproof, for correction, for instruction in righteousness, that the man of God may be complete, thoroughly equipped for every good work.
>
> 2 TIMOTHY 3:16-17 (NKJV)

> Trust in the LORD with all your heart, And lean not on your own understanding. PROVERBS 3:5 (NKJV)

> ...your faith should not be in the wisdom of men but in the power of God. 1 CORINTHIANS 2:5 (NKJV)

Action Steps

- Denounce witchcraft, the occult and all manner of devil worship.
- Repent.
- Cleanse your house and personal possessions of any occult materials or acts.
- Destroy ritualistic occult objects (crystals, astrology books, tarot cards, other god statues, witchcraft art, ingredients for spells, etc.).
- Stay away from anyone involved in occult activities.
- Make sure that Jesus Christ is the only Lord you serve.
- Know that all religions do not lead to Jehovah God.
- Trust in the Lord to help you make the right decisions. The Word of God says that by doing so, He will direct your path.

POOR ECONOMICS

Family Financial Stress

When family finances are under duress, sound financial and life decisions are often compromised. Families often experience financial trouble as a result of borderline poverty; being a second or third generation welfare recipient; having a fixed income due to disability, divorce, and separation; excessive debt; compulsive spending; bad financial decisions; and poor business decisions. Children learn through observation, and parents who complain about a lack of finances transfer this behavior onto their children. This can result in two outcomes: children do not learn any financial skills; and when they do receive money they generally have no control and run roughshod into financial ruin and the cycle begins again.

See your *Self-Assessment Workbook.*

Business Financial Stress

Business financial stress mixed with family financial stress is a recipe for disaster for both. There are times when the ebbs and flows of the business cycle place financial pressure on the business, which is not uncommon. However, unless a family has six to nine months of savings, both business and family suffer, which can lead to all kinds of poor decision-making. This can thwart the purposes of God for your life. Financial stress can cause you to make wrong decisions, lose focus, and ultimately compromise your life purpose.

Possible Problems

Here are some potential problems and consequences associated with poor economic situations:

- Three paychecks away from bankruptcy
- Bad credit problems
- Joblessness
- Filing bankruptcy

- Unable to finance/afford important expenses such as
    - Christian education
    - Home ownership
    - Giving to church and other ministries
    - Financing your God-given vision
    - Transportation
- Stress, fear, and discontentment
- Financial ruin in business
- Unable to purchase healthcare services
- Lack of stability
- Unable to care for aging parents
- Inability to make sound decisions

See your *Self-Assessment Workbook.*

Action Steps

- Pray and ask God to help you have peace, clarity of mind, and to make the right financial decisions.

> For God has not given us a spirit of fear, but of power and of love and of a sound mind. 2 TIMOTHY 1:7 (NKJV)

- Get financial intelligence (learn how to budget, save, get out of debt, invest, develop your estate plan, and obtain financial analysis). We recommend our book and CDs on *Dominating Money — Financial Intelligence.* You may also take our online *Dominating Money* course at www.workplacewisdominstitute.com.

- Do not allow financial instability or difficulty to determine your purpose. Be led by the Spirit of God and His inner witness.

TRAGIC EVENTS

Tragic events such as car accidents, home accidents, a death of a loved one, paralysis, and health tragedies are devastating. Such uncontrollable and unforeseen events may occur in your life as Satan attempts to thwart and distract you from fulfilling God's purpose. Tragic events can be devastating in many respects and affect you physically, emotionally, spiritually, and financially.

Action Steps

- Listen to the Holy Spirit's direction — that still, small voice. He will protect you and your loved ones.

> However, when He, the Spirit of truth, has come, He will guide you into all truth; for He will not speak on His own authority, but whatever He hears He will speak; and He will tell you things to come. JOHN 16:13 (NKJV)

- Realize that tragic events happen to everyone, but in all these things you are more than a conqueror through Him who loves you.

- Turn to God in your time of need. He is the God of comfort and He will give you strength to help you in your time of distress.

- Do not blame God. Remember it is not God who causes these things to happen; only good and perfect things are from Him.

> Every good gift and every perfect gift is from above, and comes down from the Father of lights, with whom there is no variation or shadow of turning. JAMES 1:17 (NKJV)

- You are commanded in the Word of God to not be ignorant of Satan's devices. He uses trials, tribulations, persecution, affliction, lust, the deceitfulness of riches, and the cares of this world to get you off your pathway to purpose.

Lest Satan should take advantage of us; for we are not ignorant of his devices. 2 CORINTHIANS 2:11 (NKJV)

Now he who received seed among the thorns is he who hears the word, and the cares of this world and the deceitfulness of riches choke the word, and he becomes unfruitful.

MATTHEW 13:22 (NKJV)

- Always remember that no matter what situation you may face, God's grace is sufficient for the victory.

The righteous cry out, and the LORD hears, And delivers them out of all their troubles. The LORD is near to those who have a broken heart, And saves such as have a contrite spirit. Many are the afflictions of the righteous, but the LORD delivers him out of them all. PSALM 34:17-19 (NKJV)

4
DAY FOUR

Obstacles on the Pathway to Purpose

CONCLUSION POINTS

Many of us have faced various obstacles along our pathway to purpose, including:

- Unstable family relationships
- Incest and sexual abuse
- Death of a loved one
- Controlling and manipulative parents or guardians
- Disinterested teachers and counselors
- Poor mentors
- Religious tolerance — witchcraft
- Unproductive work environments & relationships
- Ungodly relationships
- Substance abuse, drug abuse, and other destructive habits
- Financial stress and poor money management
- Tragic events
- Lack of godly character

It is important to know that God loves you despite your past and He will bless your life once you commit to Him. Despite the obstacles you were confronted with, there are ways to combat and deal with the issues in order to have victory.

> So be subject to God. Resist the devil [stand firm against him], and he will flee from you. JAMES 4:7 (AMP)

> Be well balanced (temperate, sober of mind), be vigilant and cautious at all times; for that enemy of yours, the devil, roams around like a lion roaring [in fierce hunger], seeking someone to seize upon and devour. Withstand him; be firm in faith [against his onset — rooted, established, strong, immovable, and determined], knowing that the same (identical) sufferings are appointed to your brotherhood (the whole body of Christians) throughout the world. And after you have suffered a little while, the God of all grace [Who imparts all blessing and favor], Who has called you to His [own] eternal glory in Christ Jesus, will Himself complete and make you what you ought to be, establish and ground you securely, and strengthen, and settle you. 1 PETER 5:8-10 (AMP)

Everyone, irrespective of their wealth, fame, and worldly success, is challenged by various stumbling blocks. At times everyone finds themselves knocked off their path to purpose. The difference between those who are successful and those who are not is that the victorious ones dust themselves off and get back on their path. In other words, they don't allow the stumbling blocks to impede or prevent them from pursuit of their life purpose. Instead, they face the mountain and move forward. Nothing stops them from fulfilling their God-given destiny.

> For a righteous man may fall seven times and rise again, But the wicked shall fall by calamity. PROVERBS 24:16 (NKJV)

> For assuredly, I say to you, whoever says to this mountain, Be removed and be cast into the sea, and does not doubt in his

> heart, but believes that those things he says will be done, he will have whatever he says. MARK 11:23 (NKJV)

> Brethren, I do not count myself to have apprehended; but one thing I do, forgetting those things which are behind and reaching forward to those things which are ahead, I press toward the goal for the prize of the upward call of God in Christ Jesus. PHILIPPIANS 3:13-14 (NKJV)

The prescription is to identify the problems that are currently hindering you from finding and staying on the pathway to your purpose. Secondly, you must begin to take the appropriate steps to rectify and resolve the issues. Know that no obstacle is too great for God. Pray for revelation in your heart that His grace is sufficient to deal with any problem that may have arisen or may arise in your life, no matter how large or small.

> And He said to me, "My grace is sufficient for you, for My strength is made perfect in weakness." Therefore most gladly I will rather boast in my infirmities, that the power of Christ may rest upon me. 2 CORINTHIANS 12:9 (NKJV)

Do not let any obstacle or one of life's challenges deter you from fulfilling your life purpose. God has called you to do great and mighty things on earth, and He is depending on you to fulfill His will for your life. You must stay on your path to purpose! Do not allow obstacles, trials, and tribulations to overcome you. *You* are an overcomer! And God expects you to maintain the victory that He has wrought over the enemy by applying His Word and resisting the enemy's traps.

> I have told you these things, so that in Me you may have [perfect] peace and confidence. In the world you have tribulation

and trials and distress and frustration; but be of good cheer [take courage; be confident, certain, undaunted]! For I have overcome the world. [I have deprived it of power to harm you and have conquered it for you.] JOHN 16:33 (AMP)

For whatever is born of God is victorious over the world; and this is the victory that conquers the world, even our faith. Who is it that is victorious over [that conquers] the world but he who believes that Jesus is the Son of God [who adheres to, trusts in, and relies on that fact]? 1 JOHN 5:4-5 (AMP)

Yet in all these things we are more than conquerors through Him who loved us. ROMANS 8:37 (NKJV)

4

DAY FOUR

Obstacles on the Pathway to Purpose

KEY POINTS

- You will face obstacles along your pathway to purpose.
- Some of the distractions that arise in your life that cause you to lose focus are self-determined and may be avoided by a change in behavior.
- You can overcome the obstacles that arise along your pathway to purpose by repenting of the mistakes you made in the past

and making a decision to research and apply God's Word and use His solutions to the problem to have victory.

- God has provided you with the grace necessary to overcome any hindrance that would impede you from fulfilling your purpose.

- Know that Satan will continually try to knock you off of your path to purpose. But remember: *he* is a defeated foe.

> Little children, you are of God [you belong to Him] and have [already] defeated and overcome them [the agents of the antichrist], because He Who lives in you is greater (mightier) than he who is in the world. 1 JOHN 4:4 (AMP)

- As a believer, you have the power of God to conquer any stumbling block placed in your pathway.

> But thanks be to God, who gives us the victory through our Lord Jesus Christ. 1 CORINTHIANS 15:57 (NKJV)

- Understand that although you may fall, you must repent, learn from the mistake, and make a decision to get back on your pathway to purpose.

> For a righteous man may fall seven times and rise again, But the wicked shall fall by calamity. PROVERBS 24:16 (NKJV)

PRAYERFUL REFLECTION

Lord, I know that You have commanded us to remain free from any bondages that would stop us from doing Your will and I thank You that whom the Son has set free is free indeed. Therefore, I am, right now, free from my past and any detrimental habits that have hindered me from fulfilling my purpose. I make a decision to follow Your Word.

I repent and ask for Your forgiveness for making ungodly decisions, harboring bitterness and resentment towards others for injustices done against me, having destructive habits, being unequally yoked in my relationships, and for allowing the negative aspects of my past to prevent me from moving forward into the great and mighty things You foreordained for me. (Philippians 3:13-15) I thank You, Father, for forgiving me and I accept Your forgiveness. I also forgive myself; and I commit to learn and apply Your Word to my life from this day forward, to be a doer of the Word of God. (James 1:22) In Jesus' name, I pray. Amen.

DAY 4: ACTION PLAN

As you fulfill God's will concerning your life, you must stay on your pathway to purpose and overcome any obstacles that would attempt to hinder you. You would be well guided to complete the following steps.

Please use the *Prayers and Daily Journal* or the *Self-Assessment Workbook* as needed to complete the following items in your action plan.

1. Give your life to the Lord or rededicate yourself back to Him. If you have already done this, consecrate yourself to the Lord to have Him help you.

2. Forgive others for the injustices that they may have done against you — intentionally and/or unintentionally.

3. Spend time in prayer to get God's will and wisdom on how to handle situations.

4. Find out what God's Word has to say about the matter and make a decision to begin to apply His principles immediately.

5. Stop destructive habits and stop making excuses for neglecting what you know you should be doing. Be led by the Spirit of God and wholeheartedly seek to do His will.

6. Remove yourself from any ungodly situations. Refrain from getting involved in activities that tempt you to engage in and distract you from doing God's will.

7. Get out of ungodly relationships. Begin to surround yourself with godly influences. Get involved in your local church.

8. Refrain from meditating or thinking about the negative events of the past. Move on. Once you accept Jesus Christ into your heart as your Lord and Savior, you are a new creation.

> Therefore, if anyone is in Christ, he is a new creation; old things have passed away; behold, all things have become new.
>
> 2 CORINTHIANS 5:17 (NKJV)

9. Going forward, if you miss the mark in an area and find yourself off your pathway, repent and immediately get back on track. Remember, no matter how many times you miss it, God loves you and He is always ready and willing to forgive you. He wants to see you victorious in every situation.

> If we confess our sins, He is faithful and just to forgive us our sins and to cleanse us from all unrighteousness.
>
> 1 JOHN 1:9 (NKJV)

10. If you find yourself off your path to purpose, redirect yourself on to the right road:
    a. Repent for the mistake
    b. Get God's Word on the situation and immediately apply His principles
    c. Forgive yourself and all others involved
    d. Find an excellent mentor
    e. Acquire the appropriate education and job training needed to fulfill your purpose
    f. Read books, trade journals, and manuals that provide the information that you need

WORKPLACE WISDOM

PURPOSE
DAY FIVE

In Day 5, the motivational gifts are introduced and the motivational gift of the Perceiver is discussed. God has called the Perceiver to intercede on the behalf of others and distinguish between right and wrong.

5

DAY FIVE

God's Unique Motivational Gifts – Introduction / Perceiver

We know a wonderful young lady named Deborah. She did not know she had a motivational gift. One day, we were sitting in a meeting and she said, "I am trying to figure out my motivational gift so I can know what my next job should be. I am not really happy in my present position." Her close friend, Sharon, immediately chimed in, "You're a Perceiver." Deborah wasn't sure; Sharon seemed certain. Deborah asked if we could help her to identify her motivational gift. She said she understood that an important key to understanding her purpose was to understand her wiring, or motivational gift.

So, we began to interview her with questions about herself and her perspective on life. After a brief questioning period, we determined that Deborah did in fact have the Perceiver motivational gift.

As we discussed the implications of this important finding, we determined that because she was a Perceiver, she excelled as a bank examiner for the Federal Reserve. She stated that whenever she was placed in a job that required her to evaluate whether something was done right or wrong, she excelled.

In fact, she remembered when she acted as an internal consultant for the bank, she could go into failing businesses and figure out what the business was doing wrong. However, once she figured out what was wrong, she had no desire to help them fix it. She just wanted to identify what was wrong. We all laughed because we knew that one of the hallmarks of a Perceiver is to determine right and wrong. She was relieved when we explained that her purpose was probably not to help them fix it. That is someone else's gift. Her gift is to determine what is wrong and once she has fulfilled her purpose, it is someone else's job to build up the business.

It was as though the lights went on in her head. She said, "I am going to be the best I can be." From that day forward she refused to accept jobs out of her purpose and God blessed her. She began to excel in her positions, and three years later she was offered and accepted the job as president of a bank examining company. She loves her job there.

HOW ARE YOU WIRED?

God made each person for a specific reason. To accomplish the desired objective, The Creator designs and equips the creation with specific properties.

The properties are tailored to fulfilling the mission — they are what distinguishes the nature of the creation. According to the Random House Dictionary of the English Language[19], *nature* is defined as the particular combination of qualities belonging to a person, animal, thing, or class by birth, origin, or constitution; native or inherited character.

So a fundamental truth to understand is that when God creates something, He equips it to specifically perform its function or purpose. Let's look at a few of God's creations.

- God gave birds the ability to fly. Therefore He designed them with wings, feathers, and aerodynamic bodies.
- God gave fish the ability to swim and live in water. Therefore He designed them with fins, gills, scales, and made them cold-blooded with the ability to withstand water pressure.

When people create things, they mirror God and also equip them to specifically perform their function and purpose.

- Cars were created to transport people and cargo across the land and therefore have wheels.
- Boats were created to transport people and cargo through waterways, therefore designed to be buoyant.
- Planes were created to transport people and cargo through the air and therefore designed aerodynamically and powerfully enough to transcend gravity.

Cars work on the ground, boats work in water, and planes work in the air. If I try to utilize a car like a boat, it will fail. It is not designed to function in that way.

Here is another fundamental truth: The nature or property of an object determines its purpose. Therefore it is possible to determine something's purpose by evaluating the nature or property of the created object.

Let's look at a few communication devices. All are made of plastic; have wiring inside; contain transistor, cellular, or computer chips; and house a power source.

- The purpose of cellular telephones is to communicate with individuals over extended distances.
- The purpose of microphones is to allow the user to communicate with multiple people over limited distances.
- The purpose of tape recorders/players is to record and project verbal communication.

The natures or properties of a cellular telephone, microphone, or tape recorder/player are different because they have different purposes. Different purposes require different wiring.

All people are made of the same substance; however, we are wired differently. Because we are wired differently, our purposes are different.

How are you wired? If you can determine how God wired you, it will give you insight into your life's purpose.

THE MOTIVATIONAL GIFTS

God created each person to handle specific tasks, and He gave each one a motivational gift. There are seven different motivational gifts. Each person operates out of the reservoir of their particular gift.

> Having then gifts differing according to the grace that is given to us, let us use them: if prophecy, let us prophesy in proportion to our faith; or ministry, let us use it in our ministering; he who teaches, in teaching; he who exhorts, in exhortation; he who gives, with liberality; he who leads, with diligence; he who shows mercy, with cheerfulness. ROMANS 12:6-8 (NKJV)

One of those seven motivational gifts represents how you are wired and what motivates you. It defines how you view the world and provides your framework. This is true whether you are a Christian or a non-Christian. Every person has a motivational gift, but it becomes enhanced and heightened when you become a Christian.

1. Perceiver
   God created the Perceiver to perceive, recognize, and distinguish the difference between right and wrong. They have an uncanny ability to determine moral and ethical issues.

2. Server
   God created the Server to help meet the practical needs of others and to spend their life in service helping other people.

3. Teacher
   God created the Teacher to disseminate and manage information. They may perform the function by teaching, researching, writing, and so forth.

4. Exhorter
   God created the Exhorter with the desire to make the lives of others more effective and successful. They are called to encourage and build people up.

5. Giver
   God created the Giver to mobilize resources for the aid and benefit of others.

6. Administrator
   God has called the Administrator to facilitate, organize, and administrate.

7. Compassion
   God has called the Compassion gift to attend to and care for the emotional needs of others.

Only One Motivational Gift?

We have found over the past twenty years that each person has only one motivational gift. It is how they see life. This does not mean that individuals cannot exhibit the characteristics of the other motivational gifts. Quite the contrary, the Bible encourages all of us to demonstrate the varied aspects of God. However, when we display characteristics outside of our individual motivational gifts, it is a learned behavior. You have to think about it or click it on to operate in it.

So, people don't have two or three motivational gifts, but they may have been strongly influenced by another motivational gift. For example, my mother is a teaching motivational gift raised by a father who was a compassion motivational gift. Therefore, she is highly developed in the area of compassion. In fact, many people who interact with her would think she is a compassion motivational gift because of the love she shows. But she is not. She views life from the perspective of a teaching motivational gift. It is easy to become confused in the area of identifying your gift. We will discuss this in detail at the end of Day 8.

You should never pigeonhole yourself in your motivational gift. In other words, don't avoid developing the positive attributes of the other gifts. You should develop your strengths to the maximum level and add the strengths of the other gifts. This will make you a powerful and developed person.

Motivational Gifts Are Not Astrology

This biblical concept of the motivational gifts is not to be confused with astrology or any other religion or New Age concept. We are not talking about being a Libra, Aries, or Sagittarius. Astrology is demonic, and it is denounced clearly in scripture:

> There shall not be found among you anyone who makes his son or his daughter pass through the fire, or one who practices witchcraft, or a soothsayer, or one who interprets omens, or a sorcerer, or one who conjures spells, or a medium, or a spiritist, or one who calls up the dead.
>
> DEUTERONOMY 18:10-11 (NKJV)

The motivational gifts are never used to predict the future. They are part of your design and wiring, and they should never to be used to determine compatibility, daily activities, or future events. Compatibility, daily activities, and future events are determined by God, not a magic list of categories.

Again, motivational gifts are given to us by God. He may anoint you for a specific task that seems to be outside of your motivational gifting. If He does, then He will give you the power and ability to complete it. Make sure you never limit your abilities or the power of God working through you.

The God-given motivational gifts are an important key to determine our purpose. They give us insight into the way God has individually designed and wired us. These gifts reveal what motivates us and shows us some of our strengths and weaknesses. The motivational gifts also reveal why we act the way we do and why others see life from a different perspective.

Fully understanding the principles of motivational gifts is not only fundamental to understanding your purpose, but it is also a major key to learning how to effectively interact in relationships with others including your spouse, children, friends, boss, co-workers, and others.

Understanding your individual motivational gift helps you determine what makes you tick (especially in the workplace), what types of jobs you can excel in, and what jobs are not suitable for you. This knowledge will help you achieve personal satisfaction and fulfillment.

PERCEIVER MOTIVATIONAL GIFT

God created the Perceiver motivational gift to perceive, recognize, and distinguish the difference between ethical right and wrong. Perceivers are wired to identify correct and incorrect behavior, and they feel obligated to expose wrong.

They have a strong moral constitution and are frequently found championing moral and ethical causes. They are outspoken, blunt, and often speak their mind without regard or reservation because they are highly opinionated.

The Perceiver's ability to be sensitive to right and wrong is vital for the effective operation of any organization or system. What would the world be like if no one helped us maintain moral and ethical integrity? Their purpose is centered around the moral principles of right and wrong.

In Romans 12:6-8, the first motivational gift is called the gift of prophecy. We choose not to use this term for the sake of the teaching because people get it mixed up with the biblical, five-fold ministry gift of prophet — one who forthtells the future.

The term *Perceiver* is a better choice of words to bring attention to how this individual is motivated. The Christian Perceiver is very sensitive to perceiving, identifying, and promoting the will of God.

Positive Characteristics of the Perceiver

1. Not a People Person
    - Very likely to be a loner
    - On Sunday after church or in their personal time, enjoys being alone
    - Will often avoid the company or assistance of others
    - Very cautious about letting people into their personal space

- Does not make friends quickly or easily, very picky and choosy about friendship
- Feels that most friendships demand a high level of tolerance
- Small circle of friends

2. Views Moral and Ethical Issues as Black or White with No Shades of Gray
    - Views everything as either right or wrong, no in between
    - Views everything as either appropriate or inappropriate, true or false

3. Extremely Sensitive to Ethical Right and Wrong
    - Quickly and correctly identifies right or wrong
    - Sees the good or bad in most situations
    - Easily distinguishes correct or incorrect behavior

4. Has a Strong Moral Constitution, Which Is the Basis for Integrity, Convictions, Actions, and Authority
    - Attempts to render justice and equity in all situations
    - For the Christian Perceiver, the Bible is the standard
    - For a non-Christian Perceiver, the laws, governments, traditions, or policies are the standard

5. Has a Strong Distaste or Hatred for Wrong
    - Has an intense hatred for evil
    - Desires to see wrong defeated and eliminated
    - Is very alert to dishonesty and reacts harshly
    - Wants things done right
    - Does not like when people lie or tell falsehoods

6. Feels Obligated to Expose Wrong
    - Often acts like the moral police
    - Is very quick to voice concerns about breaches of integrity
    - As a child, would tattletale when someone did something wrong

7. Highly Opinionated with Strong Convictions
    - Always ready to express opinions
    - Often dismisses other people's viewpoints and is very persuasive
    - Forms opinions instantaneously
    - Has opinions on everything

8. Forthright, Outspoken, and Blunt
    - Frequently speaks mind without regard or reserve
    - Will be truthful, straightforward, and candid
    - Is very transparent
    - Has difficulty beating around the bush
    - Often considered a straight shooter

9. Feels They Are Right or Correct the Majority of the Time
    - Judges right and wrong quickly; therefore, believes that their thinking and viewpoint on issues is correct
    - Demonstrates high levels of integrity and honesty
    - Because they are constantly evaluating right and wrong, they are right most of the time
    - Rarely feels wrong

10. Thinks Independently of Others
    - Will not follow the crowd in thinking or making decisions

- Will arrive at their own conclusions in their own time
- Difficult or impossible to influence, especially after their opinions have been established

11. Believes That People Should Not Compromise
    - Feels that compromise should not be an option
    - Is not wired for compromise
    - Very ethical

12. Enjoys Getting Involved in Morally or Ethically Correct Causes
    - Often becomes a spokesperson or champion for ethically and morally correct causes
    - Often involved in political and social causes (abortion, marriage, etc.)
    - Strong desire to correct injustice
    - Often fights for the rights of the underprivileged
    - Attempts to render justice and equity in all situations

13. Implements Rules, Policies, and Guidelines Very Well
    - Feels that rules and policies must be obeyed
    - Can't understand why people don't know the importance of following proper procedures and guidelines
    - Can evaluate issues very quickly

14. Makes Decisions Easily
    - Can be a quick and accurate decision maker
    - Does not necessarily need all the facts before making decisions

15. Excellent Judge of Character
    - Has an amazing ability to judge the character of people
    - Makes quick impressions of people and groups

- Has an extraordinary ability to sense when someone or something is not what it appears to be

16. Constantly Evaluates What People Say and Do
    - Scrutinizes what others say and do
    - Easily identifies faults and shortcomings in others
    - Very quick to reveal the results of their findings
    - Often communicates faults without being asked
    - Believes it is their duty to communicate faults and shortcomings to the individual
    Note: God gives the Perceiver insight into others' behavior so that the Perceiver can pray to Him on behalf of the individual. Their job is not necessarily to reveal the fault to the person, but to take the situation to God in prayer. God will occasionally give the Perceiver an opportunity to reveal the information. Perceivers are called to be intercessors.

17. Views Difficulties as Opportunities for Growth
    - Sees difficulties not as problems, but as steps to developing maturity
    - Feels problems can be avoided or minimized if people would do right

18. Has Very High Standards
    - Has an excellent understanding of correct behavior
    - Understands and easily formulates standards of behavior
    - Hard to satisfy
    - Not satisfied unless giving their best effort
    - Strong follow-up skills
    - Has difficulty tolerating inappropriate behavior

- Demonstrates high levels of integrity and honesty
- Can become easily frustrated when things are not done correctly

19. Feels That Principles Must Be Upheld
    - Operates according to the framework of principles and procedures
    - Principle-driven person
    - Comments or calls for action when principles are not maintained
    - Extends loyalty to principles rather than people

20. Enjoys Being Alone and Working Independently
    - Prefers operating independently or in small groups
    - Prefers working behind the scenes
    - Feels very comfortable not having continuous people contact at home or work

Negative Characteristics of the Perceiver

1. Can Be Very Critical
    - Tends to be judgmental of themselves and others
    - Wired to usually identify inappropriate behavior
    - Has a critical nature

2. Has Difficulty Giving Encouragement for Partial Progress
    - Often difficult to please
    - Does not easily recognize partial progress — only successful completion
    - Usually will not give praise while the work is in progress
    - Usually will not give praise or credit unless the task is performed very well

3. Often Not Accepting of Beliefs and Opinions of Others
    - Convinced he or she is always right
    - Readily embraces the concepts of justice and the wrath of God
    - Has difficulty understanding and appreciating the concept of love
    - Can take a very hard-line stance on issues
    - Will often speak mind without regard for others' feelings

4. Uncompromising and Forceful When Attempting to Get Others to Develop
    - Can be very insistent that others correct their mistakes
    - Can be very unforgiving and harbor bitterness

5. Has Problems with Poor Self-Image
    - Very critical and judgmental of self
    - Keenly aware of own faults, inadequacies, and weaknesses
    - Sometimes feels unworthy

For additional exercises, see your *Self-Assessment Workbook.*

5

DAY FIVE

God's Unique Motivational Gifts – Introduction / Perceiver

CONCLUSION POINTS

You were created for a specific God-ordained purpose. It is only when you discover your purpose, that true success may be attained. Until you get on your path to purpose, your life has limited significance.

To fulfill your purpose, God has wired you with a unique perspective and viewpoint that determines the framework from which you operate. This wiring, or motivational gift, is from God and determines the vantage point from which you perceive and respond to life. (Romans 12:6-8)

You only have one motivational gift. However, you may exhibit aspects of the other motivational gifts, which are actually learned behaviors.

Identifying your God-given motivational gift enhances your ability to understand different people. Therefore this understanding can improve your relationships with others — your spouse, children, coworkers, and friends.

Fully understanding your motivational gift is a fundamental ingredient to understanding your purpose and an integral key to effectively interacting with others.

The seven God-given motivational gifts are:

- Perceiver

- Server
- Teacher
- Exhorter
- Giver
- Administrator
- Compassion

In Day 5, we fully examined the motivational gift of Perceiver. We learned that God called Perceivers to intercede on behalf of others. Perceivers are anointed by God to distinguish between ethical right and wrong. They are vital to helping maintain moral and ethical integrity.

5

DAY FIVE

God's Unique Motivational Gifts – Introduction / Perceiver

KEY POINTS

- God has granted each of us a different vantage point from which we view life. It is found in Romans 12:6-8 and is known as the motivational gift.
- There are seven motivational gifts in operation.
- God has endowed you with one motivational gift, although you may exhibit characteristics of the other motivational gifts.
- All gifts are vital to every area of your life, including your family, church, and workplace.

- Knowing your motivational gift is a major key in identifying your purpose.
- Understanding the characteristics of the motivational gifts is critical to improving your relationships with others.

PRAYERFUL REFLECTION

Lord, I thank You for the unique way that You have wired me. I know that You have equipped me with certain abilities, talents, and gifts to accomplish a great and mighty task upon earth. I thank You that in order to fulfill my purpose, I have been endowed with a motivational gift that determines my outlook on life and my response to situations. I thank You that this knowledge will further enable me to identify my purpose while revealing my strengths and weaknesses so that I am able to interact with and understand myself and others at a higher level. In Jesus' name, I pray. Amen.

PRAYERFUL REFLECTION FOR THE PERCEIVER MOTIVATIONAL GIFT

Lord, I thank You for creating me in Your very own image with a strong intolerance for wrong; and I thank You for anointing me with the ability to discern between right and wrong at a high level.

Father, I accept this gift from You. I realize that the gifting You have placed on the inside of me is of vital importance in carrying out Your plans and purposes on earth. Therefore, I thank You for gifting me with a natural ability to judge character, make decisions easily, and implement policies and procedures well.

I count it an honor and a privilege that You have empowered me to serve as Your agent for moral and ethical integrity on earth, while calling me to intercede on behalf of others that they may fulfill Your will.

Now that I know how I am wired, I commit myself to developing and maturing in my gift. From this day forward, I will seek jobs, volunteer activities, and hobbies that will further enable me to mature in my gifting.

I realize that there are strengths and weaknesses inherent in each of the motivational gifts. Therefore, I will strive to maximize my strengths and temper my weaknesses by working to cultivate the positive attributes of the other motivational gifts into my life.

I value other people's perspectives and as I continue learning about their motivational gifts, I will embrace them, for I know each of us has a unique responsibility from You. In Jesus' name, I pray. Amen.

DAY 5: PERCEIVER ACTION PLAN

Please use the *Prayers and Daily Journal* or the *Self-Assessment Workbook* as needed to complete the following items in your action plan.

Section A

1. Perform the Perceiver self-assessment.

2. Attempt to determine if you are a Perceiver motivational gift.
    a. If yes, continue to section B, question 3 and complete the steps. (Skip section C.)

   b. If no, continue to section C, question 12 and complete the steps.
   c. If unsure, continue to complete all sections concerning the remaining motivational gifts (see Days 5-8) and complete all motivational gift self-assessments.

Section B

3. If you have successfully determined that you are a Perceiver, congratulations! You have been wired by God to perceive, recognize, and distinguish between right and wrong. That is a blessing! The identification of your motivational gift is very helpful in determining your God-given purpose.

4. Pray and thank God for how He made you; for you have been fearfully and wonderfully made. God needed you to be this way to fulfill His plans and purposes for your life.

5. Decide to accept yourself as God made you. Many people don't accept the way God made them. They desire to become another motivational gift rather than who God made them to be. That will slow up your process of development.

6. Review the characteristics of the Perceiver motivational gift and begin to observe your motivational gift in operation in your life. Write your observations in your *Prayers and Daily Journal.*
   a. Observe why and how you make decisions.
   b. Observe how you respond to situations.
   c. Observe your thought processes.
   d. Observe your natural interactions with people.

   e. If your behaviors don't line up with the general characteristics, re-evaluate yourself to determine if you need to re-identify your motivational gift.
      Remember: You do not have to perfectly match every characteristic in order to be that motivational gift.

7. Have those closest to you (spouse, parents, children, close friend) confirm your motivational gift.
   a. Have those close to you review the characteristics of the Perceiver and confirm whether you line up to them.
   b. Those close to you will have an independent opinion of how you really act.
   c. If you don't line up, start over in the identification process.

8. After confirming your gift, determine your strengths and begin to develop them at a higher level. List your strengths in your *Prayers and Daily Journal.*
   a. Go back and review the abilities, skills, and interests self-assessments and see if there is a pattern in line with your motivational gift.
   b. Have a heightened awareness of things you do well and that come easily for you.
   c. Begin to develop your strengths through mentorship, formal study or training, and/or home study, including tapes and books.

9. Recognize your weaknesses and place them in your *Prayers and Daily Journal.* These are the areas you will want to temper as you mature.
   a. Determine your weaknesses in social interaction and learn to temper or develop in those areas.

b. Recognize the areas in which you are not naturally gifted and determine how to delegate and defer to others for help.

10. Begin to identify job and work situations in which your motivational gift can be fully expressed.
    a. You may already be in the best situation to express your motivational gift.
    b. You may need to see your present job from a different perspective.
    c. It may mean slightly adjusting your present job responsibilities and duties.
    d. You may need to believe God to be reassigned to a new position in the company or to find a new job. If this is the case, be patient and allow God to direct your steps.

11. Begin to allow your gift to be expressed in your service to other people.
    a. Serve God and the body of Christ in areas that are supported by your motivational gift.
    b. Serve your family, friends, and community, and perform civic duties using your motivational gift.

Section C

If you do not possess the motivational gift of Perceiver, consider the following.

12. Identify those in your circle of family and friends who possess this motivational gift.

______________________ ______________________

______________________ ______________________

13. Study the differences in patterns and behavior between the Perceiver and yourself.
    a. The ability to understand others and effectively interact with people is a fundamental key to success.
    b. Think about times you could have misunderstood a Perceiver because you did not understand the gift.
    c. Purpose to attempt to understand the Perceiver rather than judging them.
    d. Learn to accept and not reject the perspective of the Perceiver even though it is different from your own.
    e. Pray and ask God to give you wisdom on how to properly interact with the Perceiver motivational gift.

14. Study the strong characteristics of the Perceiver motivational gift and build these characteristics into your behavior patterns.
    a. Learn the positive behaviors of the Perceiver.
    b. Avoid the negative behaviors of the Perceiver.

15. Determine ways to utilize or rely on a Perceiver to help you accomplish your goals and tasks.
    a. Determine the ways someone of this motivational gift can help compensate for your weaknesses.
    b. Determine if you should completely delegate a task to the Perceiver or just ask for advice or help.
    c. Learn to embrace each motivational gift for the unique wisdom and perspective toward life that God gave them.

WORKPLACE
WISDOM

PURPOSE

DAY SIX

In Day 6, the motivational gifts of Server and Teacher are revealed. God has called the Server to perform the practical needs of others, while the Teacher has been anointed by God to manage and disseminate information.

6

DAY SIX

God's Unique Motivational Gifts – Server / Teacher

God created the Server motivational gift to help meet the practical needs of others. They receive joy from serving others and have a built-in radar to sense what people need.

SERVER MOTIVATIONAL GIFT

The Server is a people person who loves to interact and work with people. Their purpose is centered around ministering and serving the needs of people. The Server receives joy in helping, assisting, carrying out instructions, and being of use in a variety of ways.

Positive Characteristics of the Server

1. Is a People Person
    - Draws energy from people
    - Needs to find people to help
    - On Sunday after church or in their personal time, prefers to be around people

2. Views Moral and Ethical Issues in Shades of Gray
    - Does not see things in black or white
    - Sees degrees of right and wrong depending on the situation

3. Quickly Identifies the Existing Practical Needs of Others
    - Has built-in radar for the practical needs of others
    - Very sensitive to what needs to be done
    - Always looking for what needs to be done
    - Can anticipate future needs

4. Enjoys Helping and Assisting Others
    - Loves to help meet practical needs
    - Receives joy out of serving people
    - Feels that a helping hand must be given
    - Becomes disappointed when they are not allowed to help

5. Has Difficulty Saying No When Someone Asks for Help
    - Very hard to refuse a call for help
    - Feels guilty when unable to give assistance
    - Will agree to help regardless of the circumstances

6. Will Meet the Needs of Others at the Expense of Their Own Needs
    - Will help others and neglect personal responsibilities
    - Will often assist others ahead of their own family

7. Tends to Get Overloaded and Over Involved
    - Will promise to help more than is physically possible
    - Enjoys doing as much as they can
    - Will do more than asked

8. Has a Personal Disregard for Weariness
    - Has tremendous endurance
    - Will fall out before admitting to being tired
    - Needs less sleep than the average individual

9. High Energy Level
    - Seems to have unlimited energy

10. Has One Speed: Fast Forward
    - Moves very fast
    - Likes to accomplish things quickly
    - May go faster than is necessary

11. Enjoys Physical Activity and Manual Projects More Than Mental Activity
    - Prefers working with hands
    - Often considered a fix-it person
    - Absolutely loves running errands
    - Loves going shopping

12. Prefers Short-Range Tasks to Long-Range Projects
    - Enjoys accomplishing immediate needs

- Prefers focusing on the here and now
- Prefers short-term thinking to long-range planning
- Prefers someone else to do the long-term thinking

13. Prefers Doing Multiple Tasks Simultaneously
    - Likes to do more than one thing at a time
    - Gets bored when there is not enough to do
    - Does not like to sit still; has to be doing something
    - Often will have more than one job

14. Enjoys Displaying Hospitality
    - Loves to entertain people
    - Loves to give and host parties and events
    - Will usually help clean up after parties or events
    - Loves to decorate
    - Enjoys cooking for others
    - Loves to greet and make people comfortable

15. Sensitive to the Desires, Likes, and Dislikes of People
    - Remembers special occasions, such as anniversaries and birthdays
    - Remembers favorite foods, hobbies, and interests
    - Very good at selecting gifts

16. Enthusiastic with a Positive Attitude
    - Very fun loving
    - Loves to laugh and smile
    - Loves to talk

17. Needs to Feel Appreciated
    - Must feel appreciated
    - Disheartened if appreciation is not received

- Needs approval, encouragement, and praise
- Must feel important, needed, liked, and valued

18. Prefers Not to Be in Leadership Positions
    - Can become frustrated when put in supervisory, management, or leadership positions
    - Prefers to help rather than lead
    - Prefers doing the job rather than delegating it to someone else

19. Faithful and Helpful to Leaders
    - Enjoys supporting and assisting leaders
    - Can always be counted on to help
    - Loyal and dependable

20. Prefers Not to Work Alone or in Isolation
    - Enjoys working around people
    - Does not like to work or be alone
    - Needs constant people contact
    - Does not work well behind the scenes unless there is people interaction

Negative Characteristics of the Server

1. May Sacrifice Quality For Speed
    - Not very detail oriented
    - More interested in accomplishing and completing the task than in doing it correctly
    - Thoroughness is an issue for them

2. May Neglect Duties To Help Others
    - Has difficulty managing priorities

3. Finds It Difficult to Accept Assistance from Others
    - Will not seek or receive help, resulting in delayed projects or projects of inferior quality
    - Prefers to help others rather than be helped
    - Workaholic

4. Easily Hurt When Unappreciated
    - Very sensitive to lack of appreciation
    - Will feel rejected if cannot help or assist

5. Easily Distracted
    - Has difficulty focusing on one task at a time
    - Very interested in pleasing others rather than completing the task
    - Will stop one task to help with a new task

For additional exercises, see your *Self-Assessment Workbook.*

TEACHER MOTIVATIONAL GIFT

God created the Teacher to disseminate and manage information. They are wired to process information and they enjoy explaining things to others. Teachers believe information has the intrinsic power to produce change. Teachers are usually considered analytical and intellectually developed. Most of the time they receive good grades in school and enjoy learning.

The Teacher's ability to gather and process information is vital for the effective operation of any organization or system. Their purpose is centered around the management of information.

Positive Characteristics of the Teacher

1. Not Very People Oriented
    - Not particularly people oriented
    - Does not draw energy from being around people
    - More people oriented than a Perceiver
    - Likes people but does not have to be around them
    - Has a select circle of friends (often a book is their best friend)
    - Can be a loner or homebody
    - Tends to be aloof
    - Avoids idle conversation and chitchat
    - Can feel uncomfortable in unstructured social situations

2. Views Moral and Ethical Issues in Black and White with Limited Shades of Gray
    - Sees most issues in black and white with few gray areas
    - Is very sensitive to right and wrong or truth taken out of context

3. Enjoys Studying and Doing Research
    - Loves to read and gather information
    - Enjoys general learning
    - Enjoys learning about new and varied topics
    - Easily cultivates and utilizes an extensive vocabulary
    - Naturally curious and inquisitive

4. Loves Books
    - Will usually have an extensive library
    - Will have books on a vast array of topics
    - Sometimes considers books as friends

- Prefers nonfiction to fiction

5. Enjoys Watching Documentaries, Reading Dictionaries, and Encyclopedias
    - Enjoys history and other related topics
    - When reading dictionaries or encyclopedias, will browse through other topics
    - Enjoys browsing the Internet reading about various subjects and topics

6. Loves to Give Information Even if It Is Unsolicited
    - Enjoys explaining things to others
    - Enjoys providing information
    - Will provide information or details whether asked for or not

7. Presents Information in a Systematic and Organized Format
    - Will present or explain information in an orderly method (i.e., 1, 2, 3, or A, B, C)
    - Usually takes notes in an outline form
    - Has difficulty listening to or taking notes from individuals who do not convey information in a systematic format

8. Is Considered Very Analytical and Intellectually Developed
    - Logical
    - A quick learner
    - Can absorb a lot of information and facts
    - Usually receives good grades in school
    - Has a good memory for dates and history
    - Thinks a lot, pensive

9. Validates Information by Researching the Facts
   - Is an information and fact detective
   - Feels that information must be based on legitimate facts and data
   - Becomes upset if information is used improperly or out of context
   - Uses facts rather than personal examples to illustrate a point
   - Checks out the source of knowledge and information

10. Validates Information Based on Truth
    - Feels called to reveal truth
    - Wants things done correctly

11. Thinks More Objectively Than Subjectively
    - Thinks based on facts rather than feelings
    - Can participate without becoming emotionally involved
    - Often views life with indifference or detachment
    - More interested in facts than opinions

12. Enjoys Complex Problem Solving
    - Is an excellent problem solver
    - Enjoys thinking about how to solve problems
    - Can view problems from different angles

13. Prefers Not to Be the Initial Public Contact
    - Prefers not to perform the initial sales contact
    - Does not enjoy cold sales calling

14. Very Self-Disciplined
    - Emotionally self-controlled and stable
    - Works exceptionally well without supervision

- Has a strong work ethic
- Will work until the job is completed

15. A Long-Range Thinker
    - Good at planning long-range projects
    - Can effectively think through long-term implications and problems

16. Works Well Alone, Independently, or in Groups
    - Enjoys working alone
    - Works very well behind the scenes
    - Does not need to have people contact at work
    - Can learn to work well in groups

17. More Project Oriented Than People Oriented
    - Likes to work with projects, ideas, and concepts

18. Belief Systems and Convictions Based on Careful Examination of the Facts
    - Believes information has the intrinsic power to produce transformation and reformation
    - Believes information will be effective when properly utilized

19. Average to Excellent Leadership Ability
    - Can learn to be an excellent leader
    - Can manage projects very well
    - Will sometimes view people as projects
    - A very good communicator

20. Excellent Decision Maker
    - Natural ability to analyze and make quick, effective decisions
    - Makes decisions based on information and facts rather than feelings
    - Can operate excellently under pressure

Negative Characteristics of the Teacher

1. Often Neglects the Practical Implication and Application of Information
    - More interested in the validity of the information than the practical application
    - Will communicate the information and let the individual apply it as they wish
    - Usually does not give practical suggestions and recommendations

2. Explains and Shares More Information Than Necessary
    - Usually gives more information than is asked for or needed
    - Gives unsolicited information
    - Must always teach or explain something

3. Can Develop a Know-It-All Attitude
    - Can have pride about intellectual aptitude and abilities
    - Ability to analyze quickly and knowledge of an array of topics can lead to superiority complex
    - Enjoys discussing and debating issues in order to be right most of the time

4. Can Be Judgmental and Critical
    - Can be a stickler for rules and procedures
    - Can be legalistic and inflexible
    - Does not freely give praise

5. Can Become Easily Distracted by New Projects and Interests
    - Can become bored with only a few projects
    - Sometimes loses focus when juggling multiple projects
    - Can begin new projects without bringing closure to old projects

For additional exercises, see your *Self-Assessment Workbook.*

6

DAY SIX

God's Unique Motivational Gifts – Server / Teacher

CONCLUSION POINTS

God called Servers to meet the practical needs of others. He called Teachers to manage and disseminate information. In Day 6, the Server and Teacher motivational gifts were discussed.

God anointed Servers with a built-in radar to sense what others need. They are very people oriented and enjoy physical activity. Because they derive their greatest satisfaction in life from serving others, they like to multitask and tend to get overloaded. Servers are loyal, enthusiastic, and hardworking. Their purpose is centered around ministering and serving the needs of others.

Teachers are anointed to share and disseminate information and usually present it in a systematic and organized format. They enjoy reading and complex problem solving. They are long-range thinkers and tend to be more project oriented than people oriented. They are sensitive to information being taken out of context and feel obligated to expose the truth.

6

DAY SIX

God's Unique Motivational Gifts – Server / Teacher

KEY POINTS

SERVER

- God created the gift of Server to perform the practical needs of people.
- Servers receive joy from assisting others and usually have a keen ability to sense what people need.
- Servers love to be around people and typically have a high energy level.
- Servers prefer doing multiple tasks simultaneously and short-range projects to meet immediate needs.

TEACHER

- God created the gift of Teacher to manage and disseminate information.
- Teachers usually enjoy learning and reading nonfiction.
- Teachers love to give information and tend to present information in a systematic, organized format.
- Teachers are usually self-disciplined and enjoy complex problem solving.

PRAYERFUL REFLECTION FOR THE SERVER MOTIVATIONAL GIFT

Lord, I thank You for creating me in Your own image with a strong passion for serving others; and I thank You for anointing me with the ability to discern what people need.

Father, I accept this gift. I realize that the gifting You have placed on the inside of me is vital in carrying out Your plans and purposes on earth. Therefore, I thank You for gifting me with a natural ability to assist others, display hospitality, and work well with others.

I count it an honor and a privilege that You have empowered me to serve people and to perform multiple tasks simultaneously so that I am able to get a lot accomplished.

Now that I know how I am wired, I commit myself to developing and maturing in my gift. From this day forward, I will seek jobs, volunteer activities, and hobbies that will further enable me to mature in my gifting.

I realize that there are strengths and weaknesses inherent in each of the motivational gifts. Therefore, I will strive to maximize my strengths and temper my weaknesses by working to cultivate the positive attributes of the other motivational gifts into my life.

I value other people's perspectives, and as I continue learning about their motivational gifts, I will embrace them, for I know each of us has a unique responsibility from You. In Jesus' name, I pray. Amen.

PRAYERFUL REFLECTION FOR THE TEACHER MOTIVATIONAL GIFT

Lord, I thank You for creating me in Your own image with the ability to think long-range; and I thank You for anointing me to gather, process, and disseminate information.

Father, I accept this gift. I realize that the gifting You have placed on the inside of me is vital in carrying out Your plans and purposes on earth. Therefore, I thank You for gifting me with a natural ability to study, share information, and solve complex problems.

I count it an honor and a privilege that You have empowered me with a love for reading, the ability to make good decisions, and the desire to serve people through the dissemination of vital information.

Now that I know how I am wired, I commit myself to developing and maturing in my gift. From this day forward, I will seek jobs, volunteer activities, and hobbies that will further enable me to mature in my gifting.

I realize that there are strengths and weaknesses inherent in each of the motivational gifts. Therefore, I will strive to maximize my strengths and temper my weaknesses by working to cultivate the positive attributes of the other motivational gifts into my life.

I value other people's perspectives, and as I continue learning about their motivational gifts, I will embrace them, for I know each of us has a unique responsibility from You. In Jesus' name, I pray. Amen.

DAY 6: SERVER ACTION PLAN

Section A

Please use the *Prayers and Daily Journal* or the *Self-Assessment Workbook* as needed to complete the following items in your action plan.

1. Perform the Server self-assessment.

2. Attempt to determine if you are a Server motivational gift.
   a. If yes, continue to section B, question 3 and complete the steps. (Skip section C.)
   b. If no, continue to section C, question 12 and complete the steps.
   c. If unsure, continue to complete all sections concerning the remaining motivational gifts (see Days 5-8) and complete all motivational gift self-assessments.

Section B

3. If you have successfully determined that you are a Server, congratulations! You have been wired by God to perform the practical needs of others. That is a blessing! The identification of your motivational gift is very helpful in determining your God-given purpose.

4. Pray and thank God for how He made you; for you have been

fearfully and wonderfully made. God needed you to be this way to fulfill His plans and purposes for your life.

5. Decide to accept yourself as God made you. Many people don't accept the way God made them. They desire to become another motivational gift rather than who God made them to be. That will slow up your process of development.

6. Review the characteristics of the Server motivational gift and begin to observe your motivational gift in operation in your life. Write your observations in your *Prayers and Daily Journal.*
    a. Observe why and how you make decisions.
    b. Observe how you respond to situations.
    c. Observe your thought processes.
    d. Observe your natural interactions with people.
    e. If your behaviors don't line up with the general characteristics, re-evaluate yourself to determine if you need to re-identify your motivational gift.
    Remember: You do not have to perfectly match every characteristic in order to be that motivational gift.

7. Have those closest to you (spouse, parents, children, close friend) confirm your motivational gift.
    a. Have those close to you review the characteristics of the Server and confirm whether you line up to them.
    b. Those close to you will have an independent opinion of how you really act.
    c. If you don't line up, start over in the identification process.

8. After confirming your gift, determine your strengths and

begin to develop them at a higher level. List your strengths in your *Prayers and Daily Journal.*

   a. Go back and review the abilities, skills, and interests self-assessments and see if there is a pattern in line with your motivational gift.
   b. Have a heightened awareness of things you do well and that come easily for you.
   c. Begin to develop your strengths through mentorship, formal study or training, and/or home study, including tapes and books.

9. Recognize your weaknesses and place them in your *Prayers and Daily Journal.* These are the areas you will want to temper as you mature.
   a. Determine your weaknesses in social interaction and learn to temper or develop in those areas.
   b. Recognize the areas in which you are not naturally gifted and determine how to delegate and defer to others for help.

10. Begin to identify job and work situations in which your motivational gift can be fully expressed.
   a. You may already be in the best situation to express your motivational gift.
   b. You may need to see your present job from a different perspective.
   c. It may mean slightly adjusting your present job responsibilities and duties.
   d. You may need to believe God to be reassigned to a new position in the company or to find a new job. If this is the case, be patient and allow God to direct your steps.

11. Begin to allow your gift to be expressed in your service to other people.
    a. Serve God and the body of Christ in areas that are supported by your motivational gift.
    b. Serve your family, friends, and community, and perform civic duties using your motivational gift.

Section C

If you do not possess the motivational gift of Server, consider the following.

12. Identify those in your circle of family and friends who possess this motivational gift.

____________________	____________________
____________________	____________________
____________________	____________________
____________________	____________________

13. Study the differences in patterns and behavior between the Server and yourself.
    a. The ability to understand others and effectively interact with people is a fundamental key to success.
    b. Think about times you could have misunderstood a Server because you did not understand the gift.
    c. Purpose to attempt to understand the Server rather than judging them.
    d. Learn to accept and not reject the perspective of the Server even though it is different from your own.

   e. Pray and ask God to give you wisdom on how to properly interact with the Server motivational gift.

14. Study the strong characteristics of the Server motivational gift and build these characteristics into your behavior patterns.
    a. Learn the positive behaviors of the Server.
    b. Avoid the negative behaviors of the Server.

15. Determine ways to utilize or rely on a Server to help you accomplish your goals and tasks.
    a. Determine the ways someone of this motivational gift can help compensate for your weaknesses.
    b. Determine if you should completely delegate a task to the Server or just ask for advice or help.
    c. Learn to embrace each motivational gift for the unique wisdom and perspective toward life that God gave them.

DAY 6: TEACHER ACTION PLAN

Please use the *Prayers and Daily Journal* or the *Self-Assessment Workbook* as needed to complete the following items in your action plan.

Section A

1. Perform the Teacher self-assessment.

2. Attempt to determine if you are a Teacher motivational gift.
    a. If yes, continue to section B, question 3 and complete the steps. (Skip section C.)

b. If no, continue to section C, question 12 and complete the steps.
c. If unsure, continue to complete all sections concerning the remaining motivational gifts (see Days 5-8) and complete all motivational gift self-assessments.

Section B

3. If you have successfully determined that you are a Teacher, congratulations! You have been wired by God to disseminate and manage information. That is a blessing! The identification of your motivational gift is very helpful in determining your God-given purpose.

4. Pray and thank God for how He made you; for you have been fearfully and wonderfully made. God needed you to be this way to fulfill His plans and purposes for your life.

5. Decide to accept yourself as God made you. Many people don't accept the way God made them. They desire to become another motivational gift rather than who God made them to be. That will slow up your process of development.

6. Review the characteristics of the Teacher motivational gift and begin to observe your motivational gift in operation in your life. Write your observations in your *Prayers and Daily Journal.*
   a. Observe why and how you make decisions.
   b. Observe how you respond to situations.
   c. Observe your thought processes.
   d. Observe your natural interactions with people.

   e. If your behaviors don't line up with the general characteristics, re-evaluate yourself to determine if you need to re-identify your motivational gift.
      Remember: You do not have to perfectly match every characteristic in order to be that motivational gift.

7. Have those closest to you (spouse, parents, children, close friend) confirm your motivational gift.
   a. Have those close to you review the characteristics of the Teacher and confirm whether you line up to them.
   b. Those close to you will have an independent opinion of how you really act.
   c. If you don't line up, start over in the identification process.

8. After confirming your gift, determine your strengths and begin to develop them at a higher level. List your strengths in your *Prayers and Daily Journal.*
   a. Go back and review the abilities, skills, and interests self-assessments and see if there is a pattern in line with your motivational gift.
   b. Have a heightened awareness of things you do well and that come easily for you.
   c. Begin to develop your strengths through mentorship, formal study or training, and/or home study, including tapes and books.

9. Recognize your weaknesses and place them in your *Prayers and Daily Journal.* These are the areas you will want to temper as you mature.
   a. Determine your weaknesses in social interaction and learn to temper or develop in those areas.

b. Recognize the areas in which you are not naturally gifted and determine how to delegate and defer to others for help.

10. Begin to identify job and work situations in which your motivational gift can be fully expressed.
    a. You may already be in the best situation to express your motivational gift.
    b. You may need to see your present job from a different perspective.
    c. It may mean slightly adjusting your present job responsibilities and duties.
    d. You may need to believe God to be reassigned to a new position in the company or to find a new job. If this is the case, be patient and allow God to direct your steps.

11. Begin to allow your gift to be expressed in your service to other people.
    a. Serve God and the body of Christ in areas that are supported by your motivational gift.
    b. Serve your family, friends, and community, and perform civic duties using your motivational gift.

Section C

If you do not possess the motivational gift of Teacher, consider the following.

12. Identify those in your circle of family and friends who possess this motivational gift.

_______________ _______________

______________________ ______________________

______________________ ______________________

______________________ ______________________

13. Study the differences in patterns and behavior between the Teacher and yourself.
    a. The ability to understand others and effectively interact with people is a fundamental key to success.
    b. Think about times you could have misunderstood a Teacher because you did not understand the gift.
    c. Purpose to attempt to understand the Teacher rather than judging them.
    d. Learn to accept and not reject the perspective of the Teacher even though it is different from your own.
    e. Pray and ask God to give you wisdom on how to properly interact with the Teacher motivational gift.

14. Study the strong characteristics of the Teacher motivational gift and build these characteristics into your behavior patterns.
    a. Learn the positive behaviors of the Teacher.
    b. Avoid the negative behaviors of the Teacher.

15. Determine ways to utilize or rely on a Teacher to help you accomplish your goals and tasks.
    a. Determine the ways someone of this motivational gift can help compensate for your weaknesses.
    b. Determine if you should completely delegate a task to the Teacher or just ask for advice or help.
    c. Learn to embrace each motivational gift for the unique wisdom and perspective toward life that God gave them.

WORKPLACE
WISDOM

PURPOSE

DAY SEVEN

In Day 7, the motivational gifts of Exhorter and Giver are uncovered. God has called the Exhorter to encourage and build people up, while the Giver has been anointed by God to mobilize resources for the aid and benefit of others.

7

DAY SEVEN

God's Unique Motivational Gifts – Exhorter / Giver

God created the Exhorter to help people live up to their true potential. The Exhorter encourages and builds others up because the Exhorter wants people to live a satisfying and productive life.

EXHORTER MOTIVATIONAL GIFT

Exhorters are results driven and enjoy explaining how to do something. Because Exhorters are good at giving constructive and helpful advice, they make excellent counselors.

The Exhorter's ability to encourage people, thereby making people's lives more effective and successful, is vital to the success of any organization or system. The Exhorter's purpose is centered around helping others live up to their full potential.

Positive Characteristics of the Exhorter

1. People Oriented
    - Generally considered a people person, but not always
    - Enjoys talking to people
    - Also enjoys being by themselves

2. Views Moral and Ethical Issues in Large Shades of Gray
    - Does not see issues in black and white but in large shades of gray
    - Not particularly sensitive to right and wrong or truth taken out of context
    - Allows room for mistakes
    - May ask, "What's wrong with that?" Or may say, "I don't see anything wrong with that."

3. Encourages Others to Live Up to Their Full Potential
    - Wants people to live a satisfying and productive life
    - Desires others and themselves to live up to their full and true potential
    - Can have unrealistic expectations of themselves and others

4. Prefers to See the Good in Life and to Overlook the Bad
    - Sees the good before noticing the bad, the right before the wrong
    - Sees opportunities rather than obstacles, possibilities rather than problems
    - Finds the positive in negative situations
    - Focuses on the solution rather than the problem

5. Usually Nonjudgmental

- Does not see the need to judge people
- Prefers not to frequently criticize other people
- Notices a person's positive attributes before negative ones
- Has the ability to overlook a person's flaws

6. Generally Very Outspoken and Talkative
    - Enjoys talking
    - Easily talks to strangers
    - Does not hesitate to speak what is on their heart
    - Quick to respond verbally
    - Usually got in trouble as a child for talking too much

7. An Excellent Communicator
    - Has excellent and well-developed communication skills
    - Usually an excellent speaker
    - Wonderful storyteller
    - Very good motivator and salesperson
    - Persuasive

8. Prefers to Analyze Thoughts Verbally
    - Likes to verbalize thoughts aloud to hear how they sound
    - Often talks aloud while thinking
    - Likes to have a sounding board to bounce off thoughts and ideas
    - Does not necessarily require a response from the listener; just wants to talk through ideas

9. Generally Has a Very Positive Attitude
    - Optimistic
    - Greatly admired for positive attitude and disposition

- Draws people because of positive outlook

10. Learns Right or Wrong and Truth by Experience Rather Than Research
    - Obtains information by observing life experiences
    - Views life experiences as the basis for truth
    - Determines right and wrong by discovering how something works
    - Usually does not have to validate information before it is used

11. Prefers the Practical Application of Information Rather Than Gathering and Researching
    - Wants to see information applied rather than just given for information sake
    - Believes that the key to success is properly applying information
    - More interested in putting information to work

12. How-To Person
    - Enjoys reading how-to books
    - Easily figures out how to get things done
    - Enjoys explaining how to do something

13. Action or Results Driven Rather Than Principle Driven
    - Strongly results oriented
    - Feels that projects must be completed
    - Does not like to have work or projects left uncompleted
    - Prefers to implement plans rather than develop and research them

14. Easily Recommends Specific Steps of Action to Be Followed

- Good at giving directions
- Exceptional at informing people how to get from A to Z
- Readily outlines exact methods and strategies of action or conduct

15. Wonderful Ability to Give Constructive Advice
    - Gives solid, practical advice
    - Easily sees what people should do
    - Enjoys giving advice

16. Enjoys Counseling People
    - Very good at counseling
    - Quickly identifies the issues that need to be addressed
    - Often sought out because of counseling skills
    - Shows care and concern about the personal problems of others

17. Will Quit Counseling or Giving Advice if No Change in Behavior Is Observed
    - Will not counsel people who do not take advice seriously
    - Wants to make time and effort count so will work with someone else who will act on the recommendations

18. Makes Decisions Quickly and Easily
    - Decision-making is effortless
    - Does not require large amounts of information to make a decision
    - Prefers to make decisions and implement them immediately

19. Very Good to Excellent Leadership Abilities
    - Natural leadership abilities

- Encourages others to become the best
- Easily helps others implement new ideas and concepts
- Enjoys leading others and being the boss

20. Prefers Not to Work in Isolation, but Can Work Well Independently
    - Prefers working with people than with things, systems, or abstract ideas
    - Can work for periods independently and then requires some people contact

Negative Characteristics of the Exhorter

1. Highly Opinionated and Outspoken
    - Excellent communicator with strong opinions
    - Often gets in trouble for talking without thinking first
    - Can be involved in gossip, spreading rumors, and backbiting
    - Enjoys telling people what to do, often considered bossy and feisty

2. Can Be Forceful and Interrupt Others While Giving Opinions or Advice
    - Highly opinionated and talkative
    - Can be overbearing
    - Often does not listen while others are giving their opinions

3. Tends to Take Information Out of Context to Produce Desired Effect
    - May use information and facts incorrectly to justify beliefs or behavior

- Sometimes finds it easy to justify improper ethics
- Sometimes embellishes or exaggerates to make a point
- Must be careful to avoid moral failures

4. Tends to Be Too Self-Focused
    - Always looks out for No. 1
    - Will often look out for themselves and their family before others
    - Sometimes viewed as selfish

5. Can Become Too Self-Confident
    - Sometimes thinks too highly of themselves
    - Sometimes viewed as haughty, prideful, or arrogant
    - Sometimes viewed as conceited

For additional exercises, see your *Self-Assessment Workbook.*

GIVER MOTIVATIONAL GIFT

God created the Giver motivational gift to mobilize resources for the aid and benefit of others. The Giver enjoys giving resources, money, belongings, time, and energy to fulfill unmet needs. To the Giver, the act of giving comes naturally and brings much pleasure and enjoyment.

Most Givers have natural business aptitude with an excellent ability to manage money. Many Givers are successful businesspeople in their respective communities. The Giver's ability to see and mobilize resources to meet needs is vital for the effective operation of any organization or system. The purpose of the Giver is centered around giving to the needs of others.

Positive Characteristics of the Giver

1. People Oriented
    - Friendly and gregarious
    - Sociable
    - Enjoys being around people
    - Does not have to be around people all the time

2. Views Moral and Ethical Issues in Shades of Gray
    - Does not see issues in black and white but in shades of gray
    - Usually not sensitive to right and wrong or truth taken out of context
    - Can and will sometimes justify inappropriate behavior

3. Enjoys Giving Resources, Money, Belongings, Time, and Energy to Others
    - Giving to others brings pleasure and enjoyment
    - Giving comes naturally and easily
    - Enjoys raising money and aid for worthy causes
    - Considered a very good fundraiser

4. Sensitive to the Unmet Needs of Others
    - Identifies needs before they are spoken or identified by others
    - Tremendous compassion for the unmet needs of others
    - Will attempt to bring resources to fulfill an unmet need

5. Prefers to Give Only to Legitimate Needs
    - Must validate the need before giving assistance
    - Will not give unless convinced the need is legitimate

- Thoroughly researches people or projects before contributing

6. Can Easily Identify the Resources That Need to Be Utilized
    - Able to visualize current needs and determine how they can be fulfilled
    - Able to see and mobilize resources
    - Able to identify underutilized resources and connect with unmet needs

7. Wants Contributed Resources to Be Maximized and Utilized Effectively
    - Wants to see the gift or resources fulfill a specific need
    - Feels delighted when the gift or resource is used effectively
    - Enjoys seeing the results of giving

8. Enjoys Giving Support and Aid for Others to Complete Work
    - Wants giving to go directly toward the worthy cause
    - Feels fulfilled when involved in contributions that cause a work to be completed

9. Enjoys Being the Catalyst That Causes Others to Contribute Resources
    - One of the first individuals to contribute resources for a project
    - Immediately volunteers to contribute or assist when a need is revealed

10. When Contributing, Desires to Become Part of Programs or Projects
    - Likes to become personally involved in the project

- Enjoys getting involved in the decision-making aspects of the projects to which a contribution is made

11. Desires Gifts or Resources to Be of Excellent Quality or Craftsmanship
    - Can be quite generous
    - Wants gift or resource to be unique and exceptional
    - Usually feels compelled to contribute the best
    - Often gives more than what is necessary to make sure need is fulfilled

12. Loves to Entertain and Host Affairs
    - Sees hospitality as an opportunity to contribute and meet the needs of others
    - Often involved in hosting or planning fundraisers

13. Manages Finances and Resources with Wisdom and Prudence
    - Excellent money managers
    - Rarely wastes or misspends money
    - Manages money in an organized fashion (budgets)
    - Understands how to make money work effectively
    - Usually starts saving money as a young child

14. An Excellent Negotiator
    - Often considered a deal maker
    - Excellent at finding bargains
    - Enjoys getting the best buy
    - Loves to negotiate the best value for the best price

15. Industrious and Hard Working
    - Usually diligent and hard working
    - Prefers not to be idle or lazy

16. Natural Business Aptitude
    - Very good at seeing opportunities to make money
    - Enjoys starting new businesses
    - Excellent at generating money
    - Often started businesses as children or teenagers

17. Good Leader
    - Can develop into a very good leader
    - Can become an excellent visionary
    - Enjoys leading people

18. Enjoys Being Acquainted with Very Important People (VIPs)
    - Enjoys networking with important people
    - Likes to personally know celebrities, famous, and wealthy people

19. Is Considered Wise
    - Regarded as wise, knowledgeable, and experienced
    - Not easily fooled, tricked, or deceived; not naïve or gullible

20. Works Well Independently, but Enjoys Working with People
    - Can work and think independently
    - Enjoys people contact at work
    - Works well in teams or groups

Negative Characteristics of the Giver

1. May Attempt to Manipulate or Control through Contributions
    - Sometimes gives with strings attached
    - Can sometimes be controlling and manipulating

- May want to obtain leadership roles or decision-making privileges
- Sometimes uses financial giving or gifts to get out of other responsibilities

2. Sometimes Pressures Others to Contribute
    - Can become upset when others don't see or understand the need to contribute resources
    - Will attempt to persuade others to contribute
    - Wants everyone to follow in giving

3. Can Be Offended If Contribution Is Refused
    - Will sometimes not accept no for an answer
    - Will sometimes attempt to discourage others from contributing if refused

4. Will Attempt to Make People or Organizations Dependent
    - Can become an enabler
    - Can feel important when people are dependent
    - Will sometimes use giving as a status symbol to impress others
    - Pride can be a real issue for them

5. Not Sensitive to Right and Wrong or the Facts
    - Can sometimes justify inappropriate behavior to accomplish a goal
    - May feel the end justifies the means
    - Often name drops

For additional exercises, see your *Self-Assessment Workbook.*

7 DAY SEVEN

God's Unique Motivational Gifts – Exhorter / Giver

CONCLUSION POINTS

God called Exhorters to build up people and encourage them to live up to their true potential. He called Givers to mobilize resources for the aid and benefit of others.

The Exhorter is anointed by God to give constructive and helpful advice. They are excellent communicators that thrive on explaining how to do things. Exhorters are results-oriented and prefer the practical application of information to the research of information.

The Giver is anointed by God with a natural business aptitude and is gifted in mobilizing resources. They derive great pleasure from giving resources, money, and possessions to worthy causes. Givers are excellent negotiators and tend to only contribute to legitimate needs.

7

DAY SEVEN

God's Unique Motivational Gifts – Exhorter / Giver

KEY POINTS

EXHORTER

- God created the Exhorter to help people live up to their full potential by endowing them with a keen ability to encourage and build people up.
- Exhorters tend to be talkative, outspoken people.
- Exhorters have positive attitudes and are usually nonjudgmental.
- Exhorters like to practically apply information and they are usually considered how-to people.

GIVER

- God created Givers to mobilize resources for the aid and benefit of others.
- Givers tend to be outgoing and sensitive to the unmet needs of others.
- Givers enjoy entertaining and manage their finances wisely.
- Givers are excellent negotiators with a natural aptitude for business.

PRAYERFUL REFLECTION FOR THE EXHORTER MOTIVATIONAL GIFT

Lord, I thank You for creating me in Your own image with a concern for Your people that they live up to their God-given potential; and I thank You for anointing me to communicate well.

Father, I accept this gift. I realize that the gifting You have placed inside of me is vital in carrying out Your plans and purposes on earth. Therefore, I thank You for gifting me with a natural ability to implement plans, give constructive and helpful advice, and see the good in others.

I count it an honor and a privilege that You have empowered me to build up and exhort people and help people operate in their God-given ability.

Now that I know how I am wired, I commit myself to developing and maturing in my gift. From this day forward, I will seek jobs, volunteer activities, and hobbies that will further enable me to mature in my gifting.

I realize that there are strengths and weaknesses inherent in each of the motivational gifts. Therefore, I will strive to maximize my strengths and temper my weaknesses by working to cultivate the positive attributes of the other motivational gifts into my life.

I value other people's perspectives, and as I continue learning about their motivational gifts, I will embrace them, for I know each of us has a unique responsibility from You. In Jesus' name, I pray. Amen.

PRAYERFUL REFLECTION FOR THE GIVER MOTIVATIONAL GIFT

Lord, I thank You for creating me in Your own image with the innate desire to give of my resources, money, belongings, time, and energy to aid people; and I thank You for anointing me to negotiate effectively.

Father, I accept this gift. I realize that the gifting You have placed inside of me is vital in carrying out Your plans and purposes on earth. Therefore, I thank You for gifting me with natural business savvy, an ability to recognize legitimate needs, and the ability to manage money with wisdom and prudence.

I count it an honor and a privilege that You have empowered me to be wise and gregarious in an effort to match resources with needs.

Now that I know how I am wired, I commit myself to developing and maturing in my gift. From this day forward, I will seek jobs, volunteer activities, and hobbies that will further enable me to mature in my gifting.

I realize that there are strengths and weaknesses inherent in each of the motivational gifts. Therefore, I will strive to maximize my strengths and temper my weaknesses by working to cultivate the positive attributes of the other motivational gifts into my life.

I value other people's perspectives, and as I continue learning about their motivational gifts, I will embrace them, for I know each of us has a unique responsibility from You. In Jesus' name, I pray. Amen.

DAY 7: EXHORTER ACTION PLAN

Please use the *Prayers and Daily Journal* or the *Self-Assessment Workbook* as needed to complete the following items in your action plan.

Section A

1. Perform the Exhorter self-assessment.

2. Attempt to determine if you are an Exhorter motivational gift.
    a. If yes, continue to section B, question 3 and complete the steps. (Skip section C.)
    b. If no, continue to section C, question 12 and complete the steps.
    c. If unsure, continue to complete all sections concerning the remaining motivational gifts (see Days 5-8) and complete all motivational gift self-assessments.

Section B

3. If you have successfully determined that you are an Exhorter, congratulations! You have been wired by God to encourage and build people up. That is a blessing! The identification of your motivational gift is very helpful in determining your God-given purpose.

4. Pray and thank God for how He made you; for you have been fearfully and wonderfully made. God needed you to be this way to fulfill His plans and purposes for your life.

5. Decide to accept yourself as God made you. Many people

don't accept the way God made them. They desire to become another motivational gift rather than who God made them to be. That will slow up your process of development.

6. Review the characteristics of the Exhorter motivational gift and begin to observe your motivational gift in operation in your life. Write your observations in your *Prayers and Daily Journal.*
   a. Observe why and how you make decisions.
   b. Observe how you respond to situations.
   c. Observe your thought processes.
   d. Observe your natural interactions with people.
   e. If your behaviors don't line up with the general characteristics, re-evaluate yourself to determine if you need to re-identify your motivational gift.
   Remember: You do not have to perfectly match every characteristic in order to be that motivational gift.

7. Have those closest to you (spouse, parents, children, close friend) confirm your motivational gift.
   a. Have those close to you review the characteristics of the Exhorter and confirm whether you line up to them.
   b. Those close to you will have an independent opinion of how you really act.
   c. If you don't line up, start over in the identification process.

8. After confirming your gift, determine your strengths and begin to develop them at a higher level. List your strengths in your *Prayers and Daily Journal.*
   a. Go back and review the abilities, skills, and interests self-assessments and see if there is a pattern in line with your motivational gift.

   b. Have a heightened awareness of things you do well and that come easily for you.
   c. Begin to develop your strengths through mentorship, formal study or training, and/or home study, including tapes and books.

9. Recognize your weaknesses and place them in your *Prayers and Daily Journal.* These are the areas you will want to temper as you mature.
   a. Determine your weaknesses in social interaction and learn to temper or develop in those areas.
   b. Recognize the areas in which you are not naturally gifted and determine how to delegate and defer to others for help.

10. Begin to identify job and work situations in which your motivational gift can be fully expressed.
    a. You may already be in the best situation to express your motivational gift.
    b. You may need to see your present job from a different perspective.
    c. It may mean slightly adjusting your present job responsibilities and duties.
    d. You may need to believe God to be reassigned to a new position in the company or to find a new job. If this is the case, be patient and allow God to direct your steps.

11. Begin to allow your gift to be expressed in your service to other people.
    a. Serve God and the body of Christ in areas that are supported by your motivational gift.

b. Serve your family, friends, and community, and perform civic duties using your motivational gift.

Section C

If you do not possess the motivational gift of Exhorter, consider the following.

12. Identify those in your circle of family and friends who possess this motivational gift.

_______________ _______________

_______________ _______________

_______________ _______________

_______________ _______________

13. Study the differences in patterns and behavior between the Exhorter and yourself.
    a. The ability to understand others and effectively interact with people is a fundamental key to success.
    b. Think about times you could have misunderstood an Exhorter because you did not understand the gift.
    c. Purpose to attempt to understand the Exhorter rather than judging them.
    d. Learn to accept and not reject the perspective of the Exhorter even though it is different from your own.
    e. Pray and ask God to give you wisdom on how to properly interact with the Exhorter motivational gift.

14. Study the strong characteristics of the Exhorter motivational

gift and build these characteristics into your behavior patterns.
   a. Learn the positive behaviors of the Exhorter.
   b. Avoid the negative behaviors of the Exhorter.

15. Determine ways to utilize or rely on an Exhorter to help you accomplish your goals and tasks.
    a. Determine the ways someone of this motivational gift can help compensate for your weaknesses.
    b. Determine if you should completely delegate a task to the Exhorter or just ask for advice or help.
    c. Learn to embrace each motivational gift for the unique wisdom and perspective toward life that God gave them.

DAY 7: GIVER ACTION PLAN

Please use the *Prayers and Daily Journal* or the *Self-Assessment Workbook* as needed to complete the following items in your action plan.

Section A

1. Perform the Giver self-assessment.

2. Attempt to determine if you are a Giver motivational gift.
   a. If yes, continue to section B, question 3 and complete the steps. (Skip section C.)
   b. If no, continue to section C, question 12 and complete the steps.
   c. If unsure, continue to complete all sections concerning

the remaining motivational gifts (see Days 5-8) and complete all motivational gift self-assessments.

Section B

3. If you have successfully determined that you are a Giver, congratulations! You have been wired by God to mobilize resources for the aid and benefit of others. That is a blessing! The identification of your motivational gift is very helpful in determining your God-given purpose.

4. Pray and thank God for how He made you; for you have been fearfully and wonderfully made. God needed you to be this way to fulfill His plans and purposes for your life.

5. Decide to accept yourself as God made you. Many people don't accept the way God made them. They desire to become another motivational gift rather than who God made them to be. That will slow up your process of development.

6. Review the characteristics of the Giver motivational gift and begin to observe your motivational gift in operation in your life. Write your observations in your *Prayers and Daily Journal.*
    a. Observe why and how you make decisions.
    b. Observe how you respond to situations.
    c. Observe your thought processes.
    d. Observe your natural interactions with people.
    e. If your behaviors don't line up with the general characteristics, re-evaluate yourself to determine if you need to re-identify your motivational gift.
    Remember: You do not have to perfectly match every characteristic in order to be that motivational gift.

7. Have those closest to you (spouse, parents, children, close friend) confirm your motivational gift.
    a. Have those close to you review the characteristics of the Giver and confirm whether you line up to them.
    b. Those close to you will have an independent opinion of how you really act.
    c. If you don't line up, start over in the identification process.

8. After confirming your gift, determine your strengths and begin to develop them at a higher level. List your strengths in your *Prayers and Daily Journal.*
    a. Go back and review the abilities, skills, and interests self-assessments and see if there is a pattern in line with your motivational gift.
    b. Have a heightened awareness of things you do well and that come easily for you.
    c. Begin to develop your strengths through mentorship, formal study or training, and/or home study, including tapes and books.

9. Recognize your weaknesses and place them in your *Prayers and Daily Journal.* These are the areas you will want to temper as you mature.
    a. Determine your weaknesses in social interaction and learn to temper or develop in those areas.
    b. Recognize the areas in which you are not naturally gifted and determine how to delegate and defer to others for help.

10. Begin to identify job and work situations in which your motivational gift can be fully expressed.

a. You may already be in the best situation to express your motivational gift.
b. You may need to see your present job from a different perspective.
c. It may mean slightly adjusting your present job responsibilities and duties.
d. You may need to believe God to be reassigned to a new position in the company or to find a new job. If this is the case, be patient and allow God to direct your steps.

11. Begin to allow your gift to be expressed in your service to other people.
    a. Serve God and the body of Christ in areas that are supported by your motivational gift.
    b. Serve your family, friends, and community, and perform civic duties using your motivational gift.

Section C

If you do not possess the motivational gift of Giver, consider the following.

12. Identify those in your circle of family and friends who possess this motivational gift.

____________________	____________________
____________________	____________________
____________________	____________________
____________________	____________________

13. Study the differences in patterns and behavior between the Giver and yourself.
    a. The ability to understand others and effectively interact with people is a fundamental key to success.
    b. Think about times you could have misunderstood a Giver because you did not understand the gift.
    c. Purpose to attempt to understand the Giver rather than judging them.
    d. Learn to accept and not reject the perspective of the Giver even though it is different from your own.
    e. Pray and ask God to give you wisdom on how to properly interact with the Giver motivational gift.

14. Study the strong characteristics of the Giver motivational gift and build these characteristics into your behavior patterns.
    a. Learn the positive behaviors of the Giver.
    b. Avoid the negative behaviors of the Giver.

15. Determine ways to utilize or rely on a Giver to help you accomplish your goals and tasks.
    a. Determine the ways someone of this motivational gift can help compensate for your weaknesses.
    b. Determine if you should completely delegate a task to the Giver or just ask for advice or help.
    c. Learn to embrace each motivational gift for the unique wisdom and perspective toward life that God gave them.

WORKPLACE
WISDOM

PURPOSE

DAY EIGHT

In Day 8, the motivational gifts of Administrator and Compassion are outlined. God has called the Administrator to facilitate, administrate, and organize, while the Compassion gift is anointed by God to attend to and care for the emotional needs of others. Day 8 also answers the questions and challenges often faced in attempting to narrow down your motivational gift.

8

DAY EIGHT

God's Unique Motivational Gifts – Administrator / Compassion

The Administrator is called of God to facilitate, organize, and administrate. The Administrator is great at developing and organizing effective systems. They have excellent organizational skills.

ADMINISTRATOR MOTIVATIONAL GIFT

The Administrator enjoys developing and organizing new projects. They are excellent at project planning, and they are effective delegators who enjoy leadership positions. The Administrator's ability to develop and organize projects and systems makes them a valuable member of any team. The Administrator's purpose is centered around developing systems and organizing projects.

Positive Characteristics of the Administrator

1. Not Very People Oriented
    - Enjoys people but likes projects better
    - Can sometimes view people as projects or resources needed to accomplish the goal
    - Enjoys spending personal time organizing or with family

2. Generally Views Moral and Ethical Issues in Black and White with Some Shades of Gray
    - Does not generally take a hard-line stance on moral or ethical issues
    - Does not overlook breaches of integrity

3. Tremendous Ability to Develop and Organize Projects
    - Enjoys organizing
    - Excellent organizational skills
    - Will organize themselves and others
    - Has an extreme dislike for disorganization and clutter

4. Very Systems Oriented
    - Excellent at developing and organizing effective systems
    - Thinks systematically
    - Feels comfortable working in systems
    - Likes to work and function in an organized environment
    - Takes excellent notes

5. Keenly Alert to Details
    - Detail oriented
    - Very good to dot every *i* and cross every *t*

6. Can Visualize How People and Resources Will Work Together to Accomplish a Goal
    - Has a natural ability to quickly determine what people can do well
    - Can quickly identify what resources are necessary to accomplish the task at hand
    - Enjoys coordinating resources and people to accomplish goals
    - Finds great satisfaction in achieving goals and objectives

7. Enjoys Developing and Organizing New Projects and Challenges
    - Loves new challenges and projects
    - Excellent at project planning
    - Excellent long-range planner
    - Loves variety and multitasking

8. Desires to See Projects Completed As Quickly As Possible
    - Wants to immediately implement the project plan
    - Enjoys seeing the project rolling smoothly and rapidly
    - Dislikes delays and hindrances

9. Prefers to Develop New Projects Rather Than Maintain Existing Projects
    - Enjoys starting new projects and will release them once running smoothly
    - Will lose interest in completed projects

- Does not enjoy routine or mundane tasks

10. Understands, Honors, and Respects Authority
    - Has a clear understanding of how authority functions and operates
    - Works very well when authority is clearly delineated

11. Enjoys Being in Positions of Authority and Leadership
    - Enjoys taking responsibility over people and projects
    - Feels comfortable in leadership roles

12. Will Assume Responsibility, Leadership, and/or Authority When No Leadership Is Clearly Delineated
    - Considered a "step in and take charge" individual
    - If leadership has not been identified or is ineffective, will emerge as the spontaneous leader

13. An Excellent Leader
    - Enjoys leadership positions
    - Can motivate and organize people to accomplish tasks and goals

14. An Effective Delegator
    - Can easily identify what needs to be accomplished and who can complete it
    - Enjoys distributing tasks and duties
    - Loves telling others what to do
    - Delegates well and will hold others accountable for delegated tasks
    - Has little or no problem allowing others to receive credit so that the project can be completed

15. Enjoys Supervising People
    - Can manage and supervise people very well
    - Is a Jack of all trades and master of none, which assists in supervising others
    - Has the natural ability to keep track of the assignments given to others

16. More Project Oriented Than People Oriented
    - Will put projects ahead of people
    - Accomplishing projects can become more important than the needs of the people
    - Can become so focused on the end result that they can be insensitive to people's feelings
    - Can tolerate criticism so that goals can be accomplished

17. An Excellent Decision Maker
    - Can and will make sound decisions based on the available information
    - Decision-making comes easily
    - Will attempt to make decisions for others

18. An Excellent Communicator
    - Effectively communicates ideas and concepts
    - Enjoys using charts, graphs, tables, diagrams, and flowcharts to communicate ideas

19. A Visionary — Can Envision Long-Term Benefits and Implications
    - Enjoys developing and working on long-range goals and projects
    - Has the ability to conceptualize how people and resources work together to accomplish mutual goals and objectives

20. Enjoys Working Independently
    - Hard worker
    - Enjoys working with people but can work extremely well independently
    - Does not need constant supervision to accomplish goals

Negative Characteristics of the Administrator

1. Sometimes Considered Too Bossy
    - Always attempting to tell others what to do
    - Will become upset if co-workers do not share the same vision or goals
    - Can become too focused on accomplishing the goal
    - Can be inflexible

2. Can Be Rather Controlling
    - Likes to control projects, resources, and people
    - Likes to give input into all projects
    - Wants things to be done a certain way

3. Often Views People as Resources Needed to Accomplish Goals
    - Can be insensitive to the needs of others
    - Will sometimes use people as pawns
    - Can become more interested in accomplishing goals than in the people involved

4. Tends to Work Self and Others beyond Personal Limitations
    - Will drive others and self too hard
    - Can be considered a workaholic
    - Will take on too many projects

5. Will Often Neglect Home Responsibilities to Accomplish Goals and Objectives
    - Home and work life are often out of balance
    - Has difficulty relaxing and taking vacations
    - Will sometimes neglect family and home responsibilities
    - Will often become married to the job

For additional exercises, see your *Self-Assessment Workbook.*

COMPASSION MOTIVATIONAL GIFT

God has called the Compassion motivational gift to attend to and care for the emotional needs of others. The Compassion person is perceptive and sensitive.

The Compassion motivational gift has a great desire to assist those who are emotionally distressed. They often intervene on behalf of others' hurts and problems. The Compassion motivational gift's ability to alleviate emotional stress and hurts is important in our world today. Their purpose is centered around ministering to emotions.

Positive Characteristics of the Compassion Gift

1. People Oriented
    - Loves people
    - Loves being around people; attaches to people easily
    - On Sunday after church or in their personal time, prefers to be around people
    - Loves talking to people
    - Makes friends easily; wants everyone to be their friend
    - Has a pleasant personality unless feelings are hurt

2. Views Moral and Ethical Issues in Shades of Gray
    - Does not see issues in black or white
    - Sees different degrees of right and wrong depending on the situation
    - Will react negatively when someone's feelings have been hurt

3. Perceptive and Sensitive to the Emotional Needs of Others
    - Has an intense ability to identify with what others are experiencing
    - Will read facial expressions and ask, "What's wrong?"
    - Can easily identify other people's moods and feelings

4. Extraordinary Ability to Demonstrate Care and Concern for Others
    - Great ability to exhibit love and compassion for others
    - Patient and understanding
    - Motivated to assist people to facilitate constructive relationships

5. Feels Drawn to People Who Are Suffering or in Distress
    - Will immediately notice when someone is suffering grief or misery
    - Has tremendous empathy for others
    - Will often bring home stray dogs, cats, and hurting people

6. Wants to Help to Alleviate the Emotional Stress and Hurts of Others
    - Has a great desire to assist those who are emotionally distressed
    - Intervenes on behalf of others' hurts and problems

- More concerned about mental and emotional distress than physical problems

7. Enjoys Demonstrating Acts of Mercy or Compassion
    - Loves to help the needy and downtrodden
    - Known for acts of kindness and compassion
    - A defender and crusader for moral causes

8. Grieved When Others Are Overlooked or Hurt
    - Gets upset when someone has been taken advantage of
    - Feels bad when others feel bad
    - Is pleased when good things happen to others

9. Easily Assesses the Emotional Climate of a Group or Organization
    - Can easily identify improper motives and insincerity
    - Excellent at reading body language
    - Has built-in radar system to identify ulterior motives
    - Can easily sense how people are feeling

10. Usually Noncritical and Nonjudgmental
    - Has built-in blinders that prevent them from seeing the negative side
    - Feels that being critical hurts people's feelings
    - Does not like to hear others talk negatively

11. Looks for the Best in People
    - Likes to concentrate on the good things about people
    - Prefers to overlook the bad things in people

12. Enjoys Doing Thoughtful Things for Others
    - Usually regarded as thoughtful and considerate

- Enjoys giving preference to others
- Remembers and acknowledges birthdays, anniversaries, dates of hire, etc.

13. Steers Clear of Contention, Conflict, and Confrontation
    - Generally considered non-confrontational
    - Finds it difficult to deal with and manage conflict
    - Does not handle conflict well
    - Avoids altercations and disagreements
    - Gets feelings hurt easily
    - Does not like to hurt other people's feelings
    - Does not like to argue or be involved in controversy
    - Considered a lover not a fighter

14. Attempts to Establish Peace and Harmony In Most Relationships
    - Longs for peace and agreement
    - Wants everybody to be happy

15. Considerate and Sensitive
    - Becomes upset easily
    - Can be considered thin-skinned, touchy, or delicate

16. Relies on Emotions More Than Mental Processes to Make Decisions
    - Governed by the heart rather than the head
    - Considered very emotional
    - Very affectionate
    - Cries easily
    - Has a tender heart
    - Enjoys expressing themselves in art and theater
    - Can be very creative

17. Does Not Like to Work Independently or Where There Are No People
    - Loves to work with and around people
    - Hates to work alone

18. Prefers Not to Be in Leadership Positions
    - Prefers to follow rather than lead
    - Likes to work behind the scenes rather than out in the forefront
    - Does not like giving orders and commands to others; doesn't want to hurt others' feelings

19. Prefers Not to Be Pressured or Rushed in a Duty or Undertaking
    - Has only one tempo or pace — slow forward
    - Does not like to be put in high stress situations
    - Will finish jobs, but not necessarily on schedule
    - Time is usually not a priority
    - Is a now person and lives primarily for the moment
    - Does not like to multitask
    - Prefers to focus on one job or project at a time

20. Trusting and Trustworthy
    - Usually considered truthful and sincere
    - Very trusting of people
    - Can be gullible
    - Wants to give everyone another chance
    - Will allow others to make excuses

Negative Characteristics of the Compassion Gift

1. Can Be Indecisive

- Struggles with decision-making
- Makes decisions based on feelings rather than facts or intellect
- Prefers to shift decision-making responsibilities to others

2. Vulnerable to Being Hurt by Others
    - Can sometimes be too sensitive
    - Often takes things too personally
    - Vulnerable to being hurt due to oversensitivity
    - May try to protect self by putting up walls
    - Tends to have low self-esteem

3. Frequently Reads Meaning into People's Actions and Words That May Not Exist
    - Constantly asks, "What's wrong?"
    - Frequently misjudges or misinterprets words and actions

4. May Empathize Too Much with Others' Suffering and Distress
    - Too much empathizing can be exhausting and cause loss of focus
    - Will often become too emotionally involved with people's problems

5. Depth of the Emotional Involvement Can Be Misinterpreted
    - Emotional concern can be misconstrued by the opposite sex
    - Can become too emotionally involved or attached to people

For additional exercises, see your *Self-Assessment Workbook*.

MOTIVATIONAL GIFT DETERMINATION

Now that we've had the opportunity to study all seven motivational gifts, some people may still have many unanswered questions. You may be experiencing one of these feelings:

- I don't know what my motivational gift is.
- I am two different motivational gifts.
- I am a combination of all the motivational gifts.

As we discussed in Day 5, it is important to determine specifically how you are wired by God. Once you identify how you are wired, your individual gifts and talents afford you the ability to develop and mature into your life purpose. However, if you cannot identify who you are, then there is no opportunity for focused development and your success in life will be limited.

Obstacles to Identifying Your Motivational Gift

Let's spend some time identifying possible obstacles to determining your motivational gift.

1. Some people really don't understand themselves. They are able to focus and identify strengths and weaknesses of others, but they have not developed the ability to look inward honestly and objectively to evaluate themselves. This can stem from several factors, including pride, fear, and inexperience.

2. Some individuals were reared or heavily influenced by other motivational gifts. They learned behaviors from these gifts and added the behaviors to their own. However, such behaviors are not their natural behaviors, they are learned. So they have to think about them in order to effectively do them. For example, my mother is a teaching motivational gift, and she was raised by a compassion motivational gift.

She is sensitive to the emotional needs of others, but that is a learned behavior.

3. Some individuals, especially Christians, have been trained to think and act in certain ways by church and society. When they evaluate themselves, it is from the framework in which they have been taught. Therefore they may rate themselves highly in several motivational gifts because they think it is the correct way to be or they have trained themselves to grow in those gifts. For example, someone may think that they are a Giver motivational gift because they have been trained by their pastor over the years that giving is the proper Christian thing to do. However, if they are not a true Giver motivational gift, then their acts of giving are learned behaviors rather than the natural way a Giver is motivated to see life.

4. Some individuals are underdeveloped. They may have had a difficult upbringing or experienced a tragedy that prevented them from focusing on their development, as discussed in Day 4. When a person has not been able to identify and develop their natural tendencies, it becomes difficult for them to identify their motivational gift.

5. Some individuals had their natural tendencies discouraged or even beaten out of them as children. The parent or guardian may not have recognized or understood them and tried to conform and change them into someone different than who God called them to be. This can negatively impact a person's view of themselves.

6. Some individuals are other motivational gift "wannabes."

> They feel that other people's personalities and behaviors are more desirable than their own. This can happen for a variety of reasons, ranging from low self-esteem to simply admiring the other's characteristics.

Understand that God made all of us uniquely. To feel fulfilled, you absolutely must be the best you can be. When you get sidetracked and attempt to become something or someone other than who God fashioned you to be, at best you can only have marginal success. When you fully understand who God called and created you to be and you focus all of your gifts and talents behind that, then you give yourself the opportunity to achieve your full potential.

How to Distinguish Your Motivational Gift

1. Write out the classic questions for each gift.

2. Compare and contrast each gift.

3. How to distinguish between two similar gifts.
    - Go to mentors and authority figures.
    - Observe developed gifts.
    - Have parents, spouse, and close friends help you see yourself.
    - Be honest with yourself.
    - Review your childhood.
    - Secure and listen to the two bonus CDs available with this material.

4. Pray and ask God to reveal it to you.

8
DAY EIGHT
God's Unique Motivational Gifts – Administrator / Compassion

CONCLUSION POINTS

God called Administrators to facilitate, organize, and administrate projects and systems. He called the Compassion motivational gift to attend to and care for the emotional needs of others.

God has anointed the Administrator to develop and organize effective systems in order to accomplish projects. They are highly skilled at developing and organizing new projects and have tremendous leadership ability. They communicate well and are excellent decision makers.

God has anointed the Compassion motivational gift with a keen ability to perceive the emotional needs of others. They are drawn to those in distress. They are very people oriented and derive great pleasure from demonstrating acts of mercy and compassion.

8

DAY EIGHT

God's Unique Motivational Gifts – Administrator / Compassion

KEY POINTS

ADMINISTRATOR

- God created the Administrator to facilitate, organize, and administrate.
- Administrators tend to be more project oriented than people oriented.
- Administrators are highly skilled at visualizing how people and systems work together to accomplish a goal.
- Administrators understand, respect, and honor authority.

COMPASSION

- God created the Compassion motivational gift to attend to and care for the emotional needs of others.
- The Compassion motivational gift is very people oriented and tends to be highly perceptive and sensitive to the emotional needs of others.
- The Compassion motivational gift feels drawn to people in need and enjoys doing thoughtful things for others.

PRAYERFUL REFLECTION FOR THE ADMINISTRATOR MOTIVATIONAL GIFT

Lord, I thank You for creating me in Your own image with an ability to oversee and manage multiple projects; and I thank You for anointing me to delegate and lead.

Father, I accept this gift. I realize that the gifting You have placed inside of me is vital in carrying out Your plans and purposes on earth. Therefore, I thank You for gifting me with a natural ability to develop and manage projects and people, make excellent decisions, and communicate well.

I count it an honor and a privilege that You have empowered me to be visionary with an ability to work well alone and with others.

Now that I know how I am wired, I commit myself to developing and maturing in my gift. From this day forward, I will seek jobs, volunteer activities, and hobbies that will further enable me to mature in my gifting.

I realize that there are strengths and weaknesses inherent in each of the motivational gifts. Therefore, I will strive to maximize my strengths and temper my weaknesses by working to cultivate the positive attributes of the other motivational gifts into my life.

I value other people's perspectives, and as I continue learning about their motivational gifts, I will embrace them, for I know each of us has a unique responsibility from You. In Jesus' name, I pray. Amen.

PRAYERFUL REFLECTION FOR THE COMPASSION MOTIVATIONAL GIFT

Lord, I thank You for creating me in Your own image with an innate ability to sense the emotional needs of others; and I thank You for anointing me to express myself in artistic and creative ways.

Father, I accept this gift. I realize that the gifting You have placed inside of me is vital in carrying out Your plans and purposes on earth. Therefore, I thank You for gifting me with a natural ability to care for others, do thoughtful things for others, and maintain peaceful and harmonious surroundings.

I count it an honor and a privilege that You have empowered me with a sensitive and considerate attitude.

Now that I know how I am wired, I commit myself to developing and maturing in my gift. From this day forward, I will seek jobs, volunteer activities, and hobbies that will further enable me to mature in my gifting.

I realize that there are strengths and weaknesses inherent in each of the motivational gifts. Therefore, I will strive to maximize my strengths and temper my weaknesses by working to cultivate the positive attributes of the other motivational gifts into my life.

I value other people's perspectives, and as I continue learning about their motivational gifts, I will embrace them, for I know each of us has a unique responsibility from You. In Jesus' name, I pray. Amen.

DAY 8: ADMINISTRATOR ACTION PLAN

Please use the *Prayers and Daily Journal* or the *Self-Assessment Workbook* as needed to complete the following items in your action plan.

Section A

1. Perform the Administrator self-assessment.

2. Attempt to determine if you are an Administrator motivational gift.
   a. If yes, continue to section B, question 3 and complete the steps. (Skip section C.)
   b. If no, continue to section C, question 12 and complete the steps.
   c. If unsure, continue to complete all sections concerning the remaining motivational gifts (see Days 5-8) and complete all motivational gift self-assessments.

Section B

3. If you have successfully determined that you are an Administrator, congratulations! You have been wired by God to facilitate, organize, and administrate. That is a blessing! The identification of your motivational gift is very helpful in determining your God-given purpose.

4. Pray and thank God for how He made you; for you have been fearfully and wonderfully made. God needed you to be this way to fulfill His plans and purposes for your life.

5. Decide to accept yourself as God made you. Many people don't accept the way God made them. They desire to become another motivational gift rather than who God made them to be. That will slow up your process of development.

6. Review the characteristics of the Administrator motivational

gift and begin to observe your motivational gift in operation in your life. Write your observations in your *Prayers and Daily Journal.*

a. Observe why and how you make decisions.
b. Observe how you respond to situations.
c. Observe your thought processes.
d. Observe your natural interactions with people.
e. If your behaviors don't line up with the general characteristics, re-evaluate yourself to determine if you need to re-identify your motivational gift.
Remember: You do not have to perfectly match every characteristic in order to be that motivational gift.

7. Have those closest to you (spouse, parents, children, close friend) confirm your motivational gift.
   a. Have those close to you review the characteristics of the Administrator and confirm whether you line up to them.
   b. Those close to you will have an independent opinion of how you really act.
   c. If you don't line up, start over in the identification process.

8. After confirming your gift, determine your strengths and begin to develop them at a higher level. List your strengths in your *Prayers and Daily Journal.*
   a. Go back and review the abilities, skills, and interests self-assessments and see if there is a pattern in line with your motivational gift.
   b. Have a heightened awareness of things you do well and that come easily for you.
   c. Begin to develop your strengths through mentorship,

formal study or training, and/or home study, including tapes and books.

9. Recognize your weaknesses and place them in your *Prayers and Daily Journal.* These are the areas you will want to temper as you mature.
    a. Determine your weaknesses in social interaction and learn to temper or develop in those areas.
    b. Recognize the areas in which you are not naturally gifted and determine how to delegate and defer to others for help.

10. Begin to identify job and work situations in which your motivational gift can be fully expressed.
    a. You may already be in the best situation to express your motivational gift.
    b. You may need to see your present job from a different perspective.
    c. It may mean slightly adjusting your present job responsibilities and duties.
    d. You may need to believe God to be reassigned to a new position in the company or to find a new job. If this is the case, be patient and allow God to direct your steps.

11. Begin to allow your gift to be expressed in your service to other people.
    a. Serve God and the body of Christ in areas that are supported by your motivational gift.
    b. Serve your family, friends, and community, and perform civic duties using your motivational gift.

Section C

If you do not possess the motivational gift of Administrator, consider the following.

12. Identify those in your circle of family and friends who possess this motivational gift.

    ______________________ ______________________

    ______________________ ______________________

    ______________________ ______________________

    ______________________ ______________________

13. Study the differences in patterns and behavior between the Administrator and yourself.
    a. The ability to understand others and effectively interact with people is a fundamental key to success.
    b. Think about times you could have misunderstood an Administrator because you did not understand the gift.
    c. Purpose to attempt to understand the Administrator rather than judging them.
    d. Learn to accept and not reject the perspective of the Administrator even though it is different from your own.
    e. Pray and ask God to give you wisdom on how to properly interact with the Administrator motivational gift.

14. Study the strong characteristics of the Administrator motivational gift and build these characteristics into your behavior patterns.
    a. Learn the positive behaviors of the Administrator.

   b. Avoid the negative behaviors of the Administrator.

15. Determine ways to utilize or rely on an Administrator to help you accomplish your goals and tasks.
    a. Determine the ways someone of this motivational gift can help compensate for your weaknesses.
    b. Determine if you should completely delegate a task to the Administrator or just ask for advice or help.
    c. Learn to embrace each motivational gift for the unique wisdom and perspective toward life that God gave them.

DAY 8: COMPASSION ACTION PLAN

Please use the *Prayers and Daily Journal* or the *Self-Assessment Workbook* as needed to complete the following items in your action plan.

Section A

1. Perform the Compassion motivational gift self-assessment.

2. Attempt to determine if you are a Compassion motivational gift.
    a. If yes, continue to section B, question 3 and complete the steps. (Skip section C.)
    b. If no, continue to section C, question 12 and complete the steps.
    c. If unsure, continue to complete all sections concerning the remaining motivational gifts (see Days 5-8) and complete all motivational gift self-assessments.

Section B

3. If you have successfully determined that you are a Compassion motivational gift, congratulations! You have been wired by God to attend to and care for the emotional needs of others. That is a blessing! The identification of your motivational gift is very helpful in determining your God-given purpose.

4. Pray and thank God for how He made you; for you have been fearfully and wonderfully made. God needed you to be this way to fulfill His plans and purposes for your life.

5. Decide to accept yourself as God made you. Many people don't accept the way God made them. They desire to become another motivational gift rather than who God made them to be. That will slow up your process of development.

6. Review the characteristics of the Compassion motivational gift and begin to observe your motivational gift in operation in your life. Write your observations in your *Prayers and Daily Journal.*
   a. Observe why and how you make decisions.
   b. Observe how you respond to situations.
   c. Observe your thought processes.
   d. Observe your natural interactions with people.
   e. If your behaviors don't line up with the general characteristics, re-evaluate yourself to determine if you need to re-identify your motivational gift.
   Remember: You do not have to perfectly match every characteristic in order to be that motivational gift.

7. Have those closest to you (spouse, parents, children, close friend) confirm your motivational gift.
    a. Have those close to you review the characteristics of the Compassion motivational gift and confirm whether you line up to them.
    b. Those close to you will have an independent opinion of how you really act.
    c. If you don't line up, start over in the identification process.

8. After confirming your gift, determine your strengths and begin to develop them at a higher level. List your strengths in your *Prayers and Daily Journal.*
    a. Go back and review the abilities, skills, and interests self-assessments and see if there is a pattern in line with your motivational gift.
    b. Have a heightened awareness of things you do well and that come easily for you.
    c. Begin to develop your strengths through mentorship, formal study or training, and/or home study, including tapes and books.

9. Recognize your weaknesses and place them in your *Prayers and Daily Journal.* These are the areas you will want to temper as you mature.
    a. Determine your weaknesses in social interaction and learn to temper or develop in those areas.
    b. Recognize the areas in which you are not naturally gifted and determine how to delegate and defer to others for help.

10. Begin to identify job and work situations in which your motivational gift can be fully expressed.
    a. You may already be in the best situation to express your motivational gift.
    b. You may need to see your present job from a different perspective.
    c. It may mean slightly adjusting your present job responsibilities and duties.
    d. You may need to believe God to be reassigned to a new position in the company or to find a new job. If this is the case, be patient and allow God to direct your steps.

11. Begin to allow your gift to be expressed in your service to other people.
    a. Serve God and the body of Christ in areas that are supported by your motivational gift.
    b. Serve your family, friends, and community, and perform civic duties using your motivational gift.

Section C

If you do not possess the motivational gift of Compassion, consider the following.

12. Identify those in your circle of family and friends who possess this motivational gift.

______________________	______________________
______________________	______________________
______________________	______________________

13. Study the differences in patterns and behavior between the Compassion motivational gift and yourself.
    a. The ability to understand others and effectively interact with people is a fundamental key to success.
    b. Think about times you could have misunderstood a Compassion motivational gift because you did not understand the gift.
    c. Purpose to attempt to understand the Compassion motivational gift rather than judging them.
    d. Learn to accept and not reject the perspective of the Compassion motivational gift even though it is different from your own.
    e. Pray and ask God to give you wisdom on how to properly interact with the Compassion motivational gift.

14. Study the strong characteristics of the Compassion motivational gift and build these characteristics into your behavior patterns.
    a. Learn the positive behaviors of the Compassion motivational gift.
    b. Avoid the negative behaviors of the Compassion motivational gift.

15. Determine ways to utilize or rely on a Compassion motivational gift to help you accomplish your goals and tasks.
    a. Determine the ways someone of this motivational gift can help compensate for your weaknesses.
    b. Determine if you should completely delegate a task to the Compassion motivational gift or just ask for advice or help.

c. Learn to embrace each motivational gift for the unique wisdom and perspective toward life that God gave them.

WORKPLACE WISDOM

PURPOSE

DAY NINE

By Day 9, you should have begun to discover your God-given purpose. With this exciting revelation, you will learn how important it is to become more developed and mature in your purpose. It is God's desire that you dominate to His glory in your vocation. To do this, you must mature in your life work. Not only will you please God, you will also live a satisfied and fulfilled life.

9

DAY NINE

Maturing in Your Purpose – The Adult Years

Do you remember when you were a child and the game of musical chairs was introduced? Usually there were ten chairs at the beginning of the game, placed backward and forward with eleven people. The music would start and everyone would begin to walk around the chairs just listening to the beat of the music. You knew the music would stop, but you believed you would get one of the ten chairs and not be thrown out of the game. It seemed like the ones who were just caught up in the music and not looking at the chairs with anticipation of getting their reward got beat out by the aggressive ones. The ones who paid close attention seem to get the seats.

The challenge was on when the game got down to about four chairs. It really started getting interesting. Players would sit on each other's laps and knock people and chairs over just to sit down. When you got a seat, you would hold on for dear life so no one else could get your chair.

During the course of the game, certain dynamics could be observed; everyone was given an equal chance to win, although the chairs were stacked against them. Only those who were really playing had a chance to win. The ones who paid attention to the music and the chair positioning got to keep playing. The stakes got higher each round and the success sweeter. The reward of being able to stay in the game was the spark to keep going. The intensity heightened. The pressure was on. The drive and motivation to win made the senses keen.

At the moment of truth, there was one chair and two contenders. The music was going and the competition stiff. The passion to win could not be expressed, but it was the motivator to do everything you could, everything in your power, to make the right move at the right time, to sit in the chair and win. You did what was required and you possessed the seat of victory. You won!

The adult years are like musical chairs except there is a designated chair with your name on it provided by God. When you sit in the seat of purpose — you win. Your pathway to your destiny has been confirmed.

THE PATHWAY TO PURPOSE IS A PERSONAL JOURNEY

However, finding and getting in your purpose is not magical. Many Christians believe that all they have to do is pray to God, and poof, there it is — they will find their purpose. Life is not like that and finding your purpose is not like that either. Instead, it is a journey, and on that journey, different stages will be revealed. As you mature in your purpose and walk along your path, you will begin to be successful in it.

However, if you never get on the path at all and wander through life aimlessly or if you're on someone else's path, then that becomes a major problem. God has foreordained a specific path for you to walk in. He has called you and created you specifically to greatness. He has given you gifts and abilities that only you can bring forth. No one can be you, except you, and God is counting on you to fulfill your purpose on earth.

People often will look at talented individuals and desire to become like them. In doing so, they neglect their own gifts and abilities and go through life unfulfilled and unsatisfied. Our prayer is that this will not be so with you! You have been called and ordained by God to be a great you.

THE ADULT YEARS ARE CRITICAL

The adult years, ages thirty and up, are best when you are fully developing your life purpose. There are several factors that are essential for the effective development of purpose, including job training, mentors, civic duty, and volunteering. These factors are important for maturing.

Becoming seasoned in your purpose requires diligence and discipline. It is one thing to discover your purpose, but maturing and developing your purpose into greatness requires hard work and commitment. God's best is for you to sit in *your seat* of purpose and rule and reign with Him in this life. God knows His master plan toward us.

> For I know the thoughts that I think toward you, says the LORD, thoughts of peace and not of evil, to give you a future and a hope. JEREMIAH 29:11 (NKJV)

LIFE WORK

During the mature adult years, finalize your purpose and pursue your life work. It is the work to which you dedicate yourself and achieve your greatest accomplishments. Life work reflects your God-given purpose, ruling passion, motivational gift, natural gifts, and talents. It should reveal the essence of who you are and agree with your spirit man on the inside while finding a powerful expression on the outside.

> Then I said, "I will not make mention of Him, Nor speak anymore in His name." But His word was in my heart like a burning fire Shut up in my bones; I was weary of holding it back, and I could not. JEREMIAH 20:9 (NKJV)

Your life work is determined by experience. During the young adult years, you should have been exposed to different career fields and job functions to ascertain your areas of expertise. You should have learned which skills come naturally to you and what areas you excel in. You also should have settled on the type of work which is compatible with who you are, and you should be playing to your strengths.

PREPARATION TIME IS NOT LOST TIME

As an individual makes the transition from young adulthood (ages eighteen to twenty-nine) to mature adult (ages thirty and up), their purpose should be coming into focus. Jesus Himself stepped into His purpose at the age of thirty. Moses did not enter his life purpose until he was eighty years old. Whether it is revealed early or late, it is important that your purpose be fulfilled. Preparation is never lost time. True greatness, fulfillment, and satisfaction are achieved when you live out your purpose.

God can use you effectively at any age. Some people are child prodigies and get into their purpose early, while others bloom late. The most important thing is to bloom.

No matter how old you are when you get into your purpose, know that all your preparation time will be valuable. The greater the call, the more preparation time is needed. If you feel as though you have been preparing for a long time and you're in the stage of mature adulthood, it may mean that you have a great calling on your life and the Lord is going to use you mightily in your area of purpose. Or maybe, you got off track. Get back in the flow and just understand that God can use you at any age.

The age of thirty is the average age that most individuals sit down and begin to mature in their purpose. We find many examples of individuals in the Bible who sat down in their purpose at the age of thirty, including

- Joseph as prime minister of Egypt,
- David as king of Israel, and
- Daniel as ruler over Babylon.

DISTINGUISHING THE HIGHLY DEVELOPED INDIVIDUAL

A highly developed person is one who has identified and grown in their life purpose and life service. Purpose and service evolve and its effects are seen through the incremental day by day pursuits.

The developed individual understands that their purpose and service is discovered as they step out into what God has revealed to them. By doing so, they allow God to work in their lives progressively. They make the necessary adjustments as they mature and grow in their natural gifts and abilities. This individual also recognizes their strengths and weaknesses. They know what they are good at and they focus their efforts in those areas. These individuals hone their strengths and temper their weaknesses, becoming experts in what they do. They realize that their strengths are given by God to fulfill their life purpose, so they do what is necessary to become excellent in them. By doing so, they empower themselves to mature in their purpose.

Excellent Mentors

Seasoned and developed individuals who are in their God-ordained purpose usually have excellent mentors. Such mentors are qualified and highly developed experts in their respective fields. The mentor helps to maintain focus, perfect skills, add constructive criticism, identify strengths and weaknesses, and provide accountability. An important ingredient to become a highly developed individual is interaction with mentors.

I remember my wife telling me the story about how she got involved in banking. Her mentor was the Chairman and President of the largest bank mortgage company in Michigan. He also served as the Chairman of the United Way committee that she managed.

He observed her work on the committee and decided to take her under his wing. Through his mentorship, he assisted her in identifying her ruling passion. After many meetings and a host of conversations, he facilitated her entry into commercial banking. He guided and mentored her throughout her career; and 25 years later, they both reflect upon her outstanding banking and financial career.

She now brings all of the gifts and talents that she developed and matured into the Eagan enterprises as she continues to fulfill her purpose.

Job Training

People who are developed in their purpose have studied under those who have been successful in their vocation. This can occur through direct mentoring, continuing education, by reading books or trade journals, listening to or watching tapes and videos, or pursuing specialized job training. One of the keys to success is studying under the masters and working with consultants, who, like the masters, are also industry leaders.

The developed individual has learned the systems, basic and advanced techniques, and shortcuts necessary to excel and provide an excellent product or service in their vocation. They stay current with industry changes and technological advances. By doing these things, a developed individual should get excellent evaluations on their work performance and remain at the top of their field.

For example, in the field of orthodontia, there are two different types of orthodontists — those who attend continuing education courses and those who choose not to. Those who attend the courses realize the importance of remaining abreast of current technological and medical information. Those who do not pursue continuing education stagnate. They do not improve their skill set, thereby decreasing their ability to excel in their career field.

You can tell how developed an individual is by how frequently they read books, trade journals, watch videos, and listen to tapes relevant to their field.

GOD HAS CALLED YOU TO BE A SPECIALIST

Understand that God will give you divine revelation in your career. In addition, He gives inventions and revelation knowledge to others and He expects you to sit down under their leadership and tap into the knowledge that He has empowered them with. This allows you to sit and mature in your purpose effectively by getting increased education and information. By doing so, you will become highly specialized in your work and known for providing an excellent product or service.

It is easy to identify individuals who have become specialists in their fields. For example, if you take your vehicle in for servicing, there are two types of mechanics that you may work with. One who takes an extremely long time to diagnose the problem; and after the repair of the vehicle, it will still need servicing. The other quickly and easily diagnoses and repairs the problem. The latter has studied under the experts in the industry, taken continuing education courses, matured, and developed in his life work. Both may be called of God to be auto mechanics, but those who do not perform a high-quality job have not become developed or specialized in their work. They have not taken the time necessary to sit down or mature in their purpose.

It is one thing to identify your life work and another to become good at it. To do this, it is beneficial to have consultants train you on new techniques and systems in your area and to take additional training courses.

To get a promotion or receive a salary increase on your job, you must be an expert in the job that you currently have.

Those who are excellent and specialized in their fields have higher salaries than those who are underdeveloped. This is because consumers are willing to pay increased rates to someone they know will provide them with an excellent product or service.

BRINGING GLORY TO GOD

What would the world be like if all Christians were seated in their purpose? We would be a force to be reckoned with. We would be ruling over creation as God intended in the beginning. God desires every Christian to sit in their purpose. However, Satan attempts to confuse us and make us think we don't have a purpose. When you know that you have one, he sends obstacles to try to deter you from fulfilling it.

Satan desires to see Christians wander through life aimlessly, never discovering or fulfilling their God-given purpose. He realizes that those who never identify their purpose are destroyed financially and live unsatisfied, complacent, and empty lives.

But when a Christian operates in their purpose and becomes developed and specialized in their work, they will dominate their industry. They will become industry leaders, seeking God for wisdom, knowledge, and ability in their work; financially successful, happy, and content in their lives.

FOCUSED VOLUNTEER TIME

Rather than volunteering to determine your purpose, the developed individual has learned which volunteer activities ignite their ruling passion and fuel the continued development of their natural gifts, talents, and abilities. A developed individual does not volunteer just to meet a need, but instead volunteers in the specific area where their time and effort has maximum benefits. They often volunteer in charities, trade associations, or unions. They give back to their community as a public service. They desire to utilize their gifts, talents, and abilities so that their lives can achieve the search for significance.

John D. Rockefeller is an excellent example of a highly developed individual who engaged in focused volunteer activities. After he became an industry leader, he funded the building of cathedrals worldwide. He also established foundations to help the underprivileged, raise funds for medical research, and protect the environment.

JOSEPH, A MAN WHO FULFILLED HIS PURPOSE

In the book of Genesis, chapters 37-39, we find the account of Joseph. When we are first introduced to Joseph, the son of Jacob, he is seventeen. He worked in his father's business tending sheep. As a worker, he was known for his honesty and strong work ethic.

In his early childhood years, he had dreams that revealed a part of God's plan for his life. Through these dreams, God showed him that he would be a great ruler. However, when Joseph shared his first dream with his brothers, he was faced with protest. When he shared the second dream, his brothers were angered.

One day, Joseph's father sent him out to check on his brothers, who had traveled a distance tending sheep. As Joseph approached them, they began to speak among themselves about killing him. They felt he was wrong for having a dream wherein he would be ruler over them. They sought to kill him to prevent it from coming to pass.

This is just like the devil. Your dream is revealed at an early age and family and other people try to squash it out of you. That's an obstacle.

As his brothers prepared to kill him, at the very last minute, they changed their minds and sold him into slavery. The mercy of God rescued Joseph as he faced his obstacle.

You may have gone through many difficult situations, but the mercy and grace of God has always been with you during those situations. God brought you through just as He did for Joseph.

As a young man, Joseph was sold into slavery to Potiphar, an Egyptian ruler. Once a slave, he could have given up; he could have allowed the obstacles in his life to distract him from fulfilling his purpose. Instead, he maintained an excellent attitude and continued to utilize and develop his God-given skills, talents, and abilities. He performed such high-quality work that he was promoted to become the head leader in the home, handling all of Potiphar's affairs and businesses. It is likely that Joseph was an Administrator motivational gift.

Joseph Faces an Obstacle on His Job

Later Joseph faced sexual harassment on the job. Potiphar's wife attempted to seduce him, and he rejected her. Embarrassed by the rejection, she told her husband that Joseph made sexual advances toward her, and Joseph was thrown into prison.

Despite being imprisoned, Joseph continued to maintain an upstanding attitude. He upheld his moral, ethical, and work standards. By doing so, he was recognized and God blessed the work of his hands.

Although the favor of God may have empowered Joseph to be promoted, if he had not been good at his work or if he had decided to operate in ungodly character, he would have been demoted. Getting favor to go into a door is one thing — having godly character keeps you where the favor takes you. Godly favor and character allowed him to stay in the positions he was promoted to.

> The keeper of the prison did not look into anything that was under Joseph's authority, because the LORD was with him; and whatever he did, the LORD made it prosper.
>
> GENESIS 39:23 (NKJV)

Joseph was imprisoned for many years before he was recognized by Pharaoh and elevated to the position of prime minister of Egypt. He knew there was greatness within and he decided to become excellent in his work in prison.

He made use of the time developing his abilities and skills *where he was.* He made a decision to do his work with excellence despite his work environment and the adverse situations. For that reason, when his opportunity arrived, he was prepared. God had his plan already set and when the window opened, Joseph stepped onto the path that the Lord had prepared for him before he was born. This occurred when Joseph was thirty. His assignment from Pharaoh was to be responsible for managing all of Egypt's wealth. Through his successful management, Egypt was made rich and prosperous and people from other nations came to Egypt for sustenance during the famine that followed.

> So the advice was good in the eyes of Pharaoh and in the eyes of all his servants. And Pharaoh said to his servants, "Can we find such a one as this, a man in whom is the Spirit of God?" Then Pharaoh said to Joseph, "Inasmuch as God has shown you all this, there is no one as discerning and wise as you. You shall be

> over my house, and all my people shall be ruled according to your word; only in regard to the throne will I be greater than you." And Pharaoh said to Joseph, "See, I have set you over all the land of Egypt." GENESIS 41:37-41 (NKJV)

The story of Joseph illustrates the importance of finding and knowing your purpose and not letting go of your dreams. It also shows that God's favor enabled Joseph to be promoted. Had Joseph demonstrated ungodly character, he would have lost his positions of authority. Godly character keeps you where favor takes you. By not allowing obstacles to hinder you from fulfilling your God-given destiny, you will reach heights of success and fulfillment, and that is exactly what God intends.

The same greatness that was in Joseph is in you. God has locked greatness inside of you to be released in your season. Meanwhile, He needs you to be the best that you can be.

9

DAY NINE

Maturing in Your Purpose – The Adult Years

CONCLUSION POINTS

Adulthood is one of the most exciting times for you to continue to grow and develop in your life purpose. By focusing your time and energy on the activities and opportunities that allow you to utilize your natural talents, skills, and abilities, you further enable yourself to realize your full God-given potential.

The most successful people in life are those who determine their purpose. For some, it happens early in life, typically in their thirties. This includes Jesus, Joseph, and David. However, others do not get into their life purpose until later in life, such as Moses, who began his God-given destiny in his eighties. Yet, it is important to know that God desires to use you and He wholeheartedly wants you to operate in His fullness for your life, no matter what your age. The Bible says that the gifts and calling of God are without repentance. Therefore, do just as Jesus, Joseph, Moses, and countless others have done, and do not allow adverse circumstances to hinder or prevent you from walking in God's best for your life.

> For God's gifts and His call are irrevocable. He never withdraws them when once they are given, and He does not change His mind about those to whom He gives His grace or to whom He sends His call. ROMANS 11:29 (AMP)

Remember, God has especially equipped you to do great and mighty things on earth as you fulfill your purpose.

9

DAY NINE

Maturing in Your Purpose – The Adult Years

KEY POINTS

- The greater your God-given purpose, the more preparation or time you may need in order to fulfill it.

- The adult years are pivotal in a person's life. It is during these years that God expects you to walk in the fullness of your purpose and become excellent in it.

- Maturing in your purpose requires diligence, time, patience, and prayer. The most successful and highly developed individuals recognize this and take the necessary steps to ensure their optimal success.

- To become successful and highly developed, you must:
  - Select excellent mentors
  - Participate in focused volunteer activities
  - Develop the strengths and temper the weaknesses of your motivational gift
  - Obtain advanced job training
  - Pursue continuing education opportunities

- Work with seasoned professionals and consultants who are leaders in your vocation

PRAYERFUL REFLECTION

Lord, I thank You that You have called me to do a great and mighty work on earth and I thank You that I am equipped to do this work with specific God-given talents, gifts, and abilities. I know that Your gifts and calling are without repentance, and I understand that this means no matter what my age, the awesome things You have placed on the inside of me are still there, and waiting to be put into action.

I pray that as I operate in my life work, You will be with me and anoint and prosper the work of my hands, just as you did for Joseph. I also ask for wisdom in selecting mentors who will work to keep me focused on my life purpose. Guide me in choosing volunteer activities that will engage my gifts, talents, and abilities to Your glory.

Lord, I pray that I will get a revelation of how to become a developed individual and sit down in my seat of purpose to be all that You have called me to be.

I purpose to be a blessing to others behind me. As Abraham was blessed to be a blessing, so shall I be a blessing to many because of Your favor upon my life, my preparation and excellent fulfillment of my assignment.

Father, I know that You are counting on me to be my best, so I pray that You will cause information to be made readily available to me. Show me what I need to do, and I will apply Your Word to any obstacles that may arise so that I may be a person after Your own heart. In Jesus' name, I pray. Amen.

DAY 9: ACTION PLAN

Please use the *Prayers and Daily Journal* or the *Self-Assessment Workbook* as needed to complete the following items in your action plan.

1. Pray and ask the Lord to reveal the areas that you need to mature and become more highly specialized in. Write them in your *Prayers and Daily Journal.*

2. Identify and engage highly developed mentors in your vocational area.

3. Find compatible volunteer activities that will support the growth of your natural talents, gifts, and abilities.

4. Find specific ways to increase your vocational knowledge. Place them in your *Prayers and Daily Journal* for reference. You may:
    a. Take continuing education courses
    b. Read trade journals
    c. Read books
    d. Pursue on-the-job training

5. Identify and make a list in your *Prayers and Daily Journal* of all the hobbies you may become actively involved in that will result in the maturation and development of your abilities and talents.

6. As you mature in your purpose, become a mentor to someone else to help them in their process of development.

7. Get involved in activities that will keep you abreast of technological and industry changes and advances. Involvement may include trade associations or unions. Charities may also provide the opportunity for industry growth.

WORKPLACE
WISDOM

PURPOSE

DAY TEN

There is a great life work that the Lord is counting on you to fulfill. There is also an awesome destiny that God has prepared before the foundation of the world for you to realize. So, this power-packed series concludes on Day 10 centering on how to make your purpose a reality in your life.

10

DAY TEN

Fulfilling the Greatness Within

God, the Master Creator, knew what He was doing when He created you. You are fearfully, wonderfully, and marvelously made. God thought so much of you that He created you in His image, His likeness, and in His similitude. He could think of no higher compliment than to make you like Him.

GOD'S PURPOSE

God made you with all the gifts you need. Your birth was the introduction of a brilliant plan set forth by God tailored for you to accomplish. He has created you to enjoy the good life, a full, satisfied life in Christ Jesus here on earth.

> I will praise You, for I am fearfully and wonderfully made,
> Marvelous are Your works, And that my soul knows very well.
>
> PSALM 139:14 (NKJV)

You have arrived at Day 10! That is awesome! Let us take a quick look at where we have been for the last nine days.

On Day 1, we talked about purpose and the fact that God created and uniquely designed you for a purpose. There is something special that He placed on the inside of you that He wants you to accomplish. He has given you His power and ability to do the very thing He created and called you to do. God would not leave you purposeless. He loves you so very much, and He planned your destiny far in advance.

On Day 2, we covered the formative years and discussed the fact that God wants you to grow and develop in your God-given gifts and abilities. God's best is that you identify, grow, and develop at an early age, supported by the observation, training, and influence of parents, teachers, and mentors.

Education, exposure, and moral and character development are pivotal. In addition, job experiences, hobbies, civic duties, and volunteer activities are designed to help you cultivate your gifts. Development in each of these areas leads to an understanding of your life work.

On Day 3, we discussed how God wants you to continue to develop during your young adult years by taking on different jobs and engaging in different work experiences so that you get a true idea of what your gifts and talents are. At this time you identify your preferences and ruling passion. Jeremiah referred to his ruling passion as "fire shut up in his bones." You must be guided by your ruling passion — it is the fire on the inside and unless you allow it to be realized, you will feel unfulfilled.

> Then I said, "I will not make mention of Him, Nor speak anymore in His name." But His word was in my heart like a

> burning fire Shut up in my bones; I was weary of holding it back, and I could not. JEREMIAH 20:9 (NKJV)

On Day 4, obstacles that may have impeded your growth and development were delineated. We learned that God always holds your place on the path to purpose because His calling is without repentance.

Although we could not cover every obstacle that might have stunted your growth, we did identify one-hundred twelve. Your assignment was to pray and ask God to show you the specific obstacle(s) that impeded your progress. We are absolutely certain that He has not only heard your prayers but is answering them.

> Now this is the confidence that we have in Him, that if we ask anything according to His will, He hears us. And if we know that He hears us, whatever we ask, we know that we have the petitions that we have asked of Him.
>
> 1 JOHN 5:14-15 (NKJV)

On Day 5 through Day 8, we examined the seven motivational gifts. We learned that they shed light on the manner in which we see the world. We like to say it is how you are wired by God to fulfill your purpose with a particular worldview.

Whether your gift is that of a Teacher, Compassion, Administrator, Perceiver, Exhorter, Server, or Giver, you need to know your motivational gift because your primary behavioral response evolves out of it. You think from your motivational gift. It drives your internal behavioral mechanisms and is designed by God to keep you on your path to purpose.

Knowing your motivational gift is pivotal in helping you make critical decisions to fulfill the purpose God intended for you and to have a full and satisfied life. Each gift has an important function. The Perceiver is called to be an intercessor, the Server is the helping hands, the Teacher disseminates information, the Exhorter builds people up, the Giver mobilizes resources, the Administrator organizes excellently, and the Compassion motivational gift has a heart for people.

In our unscientific research, we believe that 40 percent of all people are Compassion motivational gifts. When we think of who God is, that seems right — because God is Love.

> And we have known and believed the love that God has for us. God is love, and he who abides in love abides in God, and God in him. 1 JOHN 4:16 (NKJV)

Many people do not know their motivational gift or simply cannot determine it. Some feel they are a combination of gifts. But God has gifted each of us with one motivational gift, although we may exhibit characteristics of other gifts. Despite this, our worldview and the framework from which we make decisions is based on one motivational gift.

On Day 9, we focused on maturing in your purpose and growing it throughout your adult years. This results in your being successful which allows you to be a tremendous blessing to people from all walks of life. You become a valuable gift and pour out of the reservoir of your life.

In Day 10, we will discuss how your life reflects a message to the world. As you mature and develop in your life purpose, your life message evolves and changes over the course of time. Your life purpose is defined by your life work and it is what you dedicate your life to and your life service/ministry.

God has given you a purpose. It is up to you to accept it, understand it, and fulfill it even if no one helps or aids you. That is an almost impossible thought because God never leaves His children helpless! He will always find someone to help you identify your life purpose and fulfill it all along the path.

> And I will pray the Father, and He will give you another Helper, that He may abide with you forever.
>
> JOHN 14:16 (NKJV)

LIFE WORK

Work is a gift from God. When you operate in the life work that God has called you to, you allow all of the gifts He has placed inside of you to be showcased — your inner greatness is revealed. This is why the enemy seeks to deceive people into stepping out of their purpose or being lackadaisical in their work.

> And also that every man should eat and drink and enjoy the good of all his labor — it is the gift of God.
>
> ECCLESIASTES 3:13 (NKJV)

Remember, your life work is the work to which you dedicate yourself and achieve your greatest accomplishments. Your God-given purpose encompasses your life work, ruling passion, motivational gift, natural gifts, and talents. It is during your young adult years, that you become anchored. You should have been exposed to different career fields, hobbies, volunteer experiences, and job functions to ascertain and cement your areas of expertise.

The combination of knowing these ingredients takes you a considerable distance toward understanding and manifesting your purpose. For example, if at the age of twelve you discover that you have a knack for numbers and it is easy for you to calculate in your head, then you have identified a gift. If the gift is fully developed, it can become an awesome talent, which can be very useful in life.

Further, if your love for mathematics is combined with a teaching motivational gift, then being a speaker, teacher, researcher, lecturer, author, or scientist would all be highly complementary to your natural and developed gift. Consider Albert Einstein whose life encompassed all of the above.

Let's look at another example of someone with a gift for mathematics. But let's say that person is a Giver. Such a person would probably volunteer time and money to help a charitable organization; and they would probably sit on the finance committee as well. We can also see the mathematician/Giver being excellent in business dealings. That person would be similar to John D. Rockefeller, who had a natural acumen for business and adding numbers in his head.

One last example. Couple the same gift of mathematics with the motivational gift of Perceiver. Such a person might work as an auditor, bank examiner, accountant, commercial lender, mortgage lender, or any other type of work that is detail oriented and discerning of right and wrong. Consider Deborah who we discussed earlier. It can be plainly seen that gifts plus talents plus motivational gift can result in very different life work. Same gift, different motivational gift equals different career.

Those who are super wealthy have narrowed their work and mastered one primary trade. This is God's best. According to Thomas Stanley, author of *The Millionaire Mind*, only 5 percent of America's wealthy have inherited their wealth. The rest have earned it.[20] This is good news because it means that we have a 95 percent opportunity to use the principles of God and work to become financially blessed, *if* we are single-minded. We must be focused.

There should be one phrase that defines your life work.

Consider such world-renowned people as:

- Jesus Christ, Savior of the world
- Oprah Winfrey, talk show host
- Tiger Woods, master golfer
- John D. Rockefeller, oil magnate and philanthroper
- Mary Kay, cosmetic entrepreneur
- Warren Buffet, investment strategist

- Michael Jordan, professional basketball player
- George W. Bush, politician
- Ben Carson, pediatric neurosurgeon
- John Maxwell, New York Times best-selling author
- Zig Ziglar, motivational speaker

What is that one phrase which will define your life? What will you be known for? Something that others consider you to be expert in.

Child Prodigies

Defining your life work can happen at an early age. There are many examples of individuals who developed their God-given gifts and became talented while young, as early as age three or four.

God is no respecter of persons. In fact, He designed you to determine your purpose at an early age so that you may enjoy the fullness of everything He has created for you.

Consider Michael Jackson who was a singer with the Jackson Five. His mother discovered him while singing in his bedroom at the age of five. She told her husband; Michael was added to the group, and the rest is history. Formal education may not have played a factor in his success, but he had a gift that was honed into a talent, and he became known worldwide after getting into his life work at an early age.

Wolfgang Mozart, the great composer, is another example. He received such outstanding training that by the age of six, he was a novice composer. In addition, he was a very accomplished piano player. And what about Shirley Temple? She was discovered in a dancing school and began appearing in movies at the age of three-and-a-half. In each of these cases, parents observed their children and allowed their child's gift to be developed into a talent.

A TALENT IS A DEVELOPED GIFT

A talent is a developed gift. Your talent is observable. You may have a gift for playing the piano, but if you never develop and mature in that gift, you will not be considered talented. Or at best, labeled as raw talent and who wants that! Tiger Woods has a gift for swinging the golf club. But if he had not spent countless hours developing in that area, he would not be considered a talented golfer, but just another hacker.

You must identify your gifts and then hone them so that you may mature in that area. This is how you become highly developed and obtain great skills. A gift is rarely recognized unless it is developed into a talent.

If you do not develop your gift into a talent, you will be frustrated and feel unfulfilled in your life work. This is why it is critical to discover and get into it.

LIFE SERVICE/MINISTRY

While you are developing your life work, you must simultaneously be developing your life service/ministry. Life service/ministry is the way you spend time qualitatively adding to the lives of others.

LIFE SERVICE

We spend over 70 percent of our waking time involved in workplace related activity. If we are not effective in our life work – we will not feel fulfilled. Furthermore, success in our work is not enough. We must also be effective in our service outside of work. We call it your life service.

Life service is our ministry into the lives of other people. We should minister to God, our family, our church, our workplace, our civic activities, and in all areas of our lives. Until life work and life service are combined and we are positively impacting others' lives, we will not feel a sense of contentment. If we are out of balance in one area, we will be frustrated.

Does Being Called Mean Going into the Ministry?

In order to perform life service/ministry, you do not have to give up your secular job and go into the five-fold ministry. (Ephesians 4:11) If everyone did this, the world would collapse. The Church would suffer since no one would earn money to contribute to it. How would the Church equip the saints to carry God's Word to the world?

Everyone is important to God. Every job is important to God and not everyone is called to the five-fold ministry. God needs you to fulfill the unique call that He has placed on your life. You are anointed to do what He has called you to do, whether that means working as an architect, clergyman, entrepreneur, chemist, gynecologist, or housewife.

Life Service/Ministry — Adding to the Lives of Others

Your life service/ministry has six primary components, which are hierarchical in nature. The first is to God, then family, church, workplace, community, and lastly civic duty. The overall point is that fulfillment of purpose encompasses a relationship with God and service to others.

Service to God

When you are in your purpose, God becomes your advocate and way maker. What a partner! This is exciting because there is nothing that is impossible for God. The only thing He needs us to do is mount ourselves up and pursue His plans and purpose for our lives. By doing this, God opens doors and makes resources available to us.

> But He said, "The things which are impossible with men are possible with God." LUKE 18:27 (NKJV)

We need godly people in every walk of life. Get busy doing what God has called you to do. God needs you! This is the hour —- this is the time for you to rise up and take your rightful place.

Every believer must go beyond salvation and develop a strong relationship with God through His Son, Jesus Christ. Your personal relationship with God must permeate every aspect of your life such that it becomes a service to God. It is a service of love and not duty. It is rendered out of a sincere, genuine, and heartfelt love for God.

Your service includes daily prayer time, daily study of your Bible, and daily meditative time with Him. Trust and believe that God's Word is true and fundamental. Once you have established your service to the Lord, you will be ready to demonstrate the love of God to people.

Your greatest witness of God to the world is how you live. Your life should glorify God and show God's character to others, including His love and forgiveness. The Bible admonishes us to be doers of the Word and not hearers only. Therefore, your life service/ministry should be an overflow of God's goodness, mercy, and love operating in your own life.

> Therefore, whether you eat or drink, or whatever you do, do all to the glory of God. 1 CORINTHIANS 10:31 (NKJV)

> But be doers of the word, and not hearers only, deceiving yourselves. JAMES 1:22 (NKJV)

Service to Family

The first group God would send you to is your family — His first institution. You must use your gifts, talents, financial resources, and abilities to help your family. Some examples of serving your family are handling the finances, addressing their spiritual and emotional needs, and meeting practical needs.

> But if anyone does not provide for his own, and especially for those of his household, he has denied the faith and is worse than an unbeliever. 1 TIMOTHY 5:8 (NKJV)

Service to the Church

You must support the body of Christ so the Lord's work can grow. Gifts, talents, financial resources, and abilities should be used to serve in your local church. For instance, part-time missionary work, serving in auxiliaries such as deacon board, usher board, building fundraisers, and so forth are all excellent ways to serve. Believers should volunteer at the house of God *first* before meeting the needs of secular charitable organizations. Christians should financially support the church ahead of other non-profit organizations.

> Therefore, as we have opportunity, let us do good to all, especially to those who are of the household of faith.
>
> GALATIANS 6:10 (NKJV)

Service at our Workplace

Work is important to God. Billy Graham said, "I believe one of the next great moves of God is going to be through believers in the workplace." Work allows you to fulfill the greatness God has placed within you. Life service at your workplace is a major component of your life purpose. You minister to others at your workplace by providing an excellent product or service and by acting as a conduit of the love of God to your employer, supervisors, co-workers, clients, vendors, and competitors.

This can be done through kindness and acts of compassion, a simple smile, saying hello, expressing godly ethics and character, praying for others, or asking how you might help other people. It is also imperative that a Christian share Christ in their workplace. One of the best ways is to be a godly example.

> But the fruit of the Spirit is love, joy, peace, longsuffering, kindness, goodness, faithfulness, gentleness, self-control. Against such there is no law. GALATIANS 5:22-23 (NKJV)

Community Service

Use your gifts, talents, and abilities to serve your community for the greater good. This includes serving in the political arena — local, regional, or national. In addition, serving in non-profit organizations, trade associations, community organizations, and so forth is a valuable service to the community.

In past decades, established citizens were concerned about their communities and dedicated their time and resources to it. For example, Henry Ford II was concerned about his environment and built the Renaissance Center in downtown Detroit to benefit the local community and local economy. Today, many people are inwardly focused and do not consider the greater good of the community.

> ...with goodwill doing service, as to the Lord, and not to men.
> EPHESIANS 6:7 (NKJV)

Civic Duty

Civic duty includes voting, jury duty, military duty, and those other duties for which your citizenship allows you to enjoy certain rights. Your civic duty demands that you vote and participate in the electoral process. Because Christians did not vote in large numbers for those who would support godly principles, prayer was taken out of schools and there is now a debate against taking "In God We Trust" off of the U.S. currency. We must get involved in the judicial process — all the way up to the U.S. Supreme Court — to protect the rights of Christians and defend our nation against ungodliness.

You will give an account to God for all decisions that you make. To whom much is given, much is required.

> So then each of us shall give account of himself to God.
>
> ROMANS 14:12 (NKJV)

LIFE MESSAGE

Life message is a communication. Your life message is the conscious or unconscious statement of the substance of your life. It is the compilation of your life expressed in your articulation, agenda, and priorities. Each person is given a purpose by God, but your life message is what you choose to live out. Every Christian is called by God to communicate the saving knowledge of Christ Jesus to a dying world. However, your life message is specifically tailored to your life.

Adults who understand their purpose have a unique opportunity and responsibility to impact society. Having matured spiritually, vocationally, intellectually, socially and physically it is now time to turn to your life message.

Everyone Has a Life Message

You can walk up to a complete stranger and talk to them for about thirty minutes and discover their life message. This is because the Word of God says that what is on the inside comes out; out of the abundance of the heart the mouth speaks. You will be a billboard for whatever you are practicing. Whether you know it or not, you have a life message.

> For out of the abundance of the heart the mouth speaks.
>
> MATTHEW 12:34B (NKJV)

Your life message can be nonverbal and yet powerfully communicated. For example, my husband observed me for three years before he ever approached me. If I had been living an ungodly life, he would have said that life message was not for him. This is why you must be sure that your life message bespeaks a godly heritage.

Generally, a life message is developed in the early developmental years of a child. Early on, parents are imparting their life message onto their child. It is during the preadolescent and adolescent years that youth begin to develop their own life message. Godly parents who have studied and lived the Word of God have placed a powerful life-giving tool in the hearts and minds of their children, which will keep them through eternity if they follow Christ. In either case, a life message is developing. By adulthood, a significant message has been established.

A life message is engineered, whether good or bad, noble or ignoble, godly or ungodly. It is always interesting to us as we travel around the world to learn that so many adults do not understand the concept of life message or know that their life is speaking a message.

Your Purpose Does Not Change, but Your Life Message Can

Your life message is not static. It grows and evolves as you grow. Your purpose will not change. It was established before the foundation of the world. Yet your life message may change based on what you do. For example, a drug dealer who uses his God-given talents of administration or selling to distribute drugs communicates immorality and illegality with his life message. But the same person can turn his life around and get a legitimate job, serve God, and bless his community. Clearly, such an individual has changed his life message. Although, your life message can change, your life purpose cannot because God does not change His mind, nor is there any changeability in Him.

> Jesus Christ is the same yesterday, today, and forever.
>
> HEBREWS 13:8 (NKJV)

> For I am the LORD, I do not change; Therefore, you are not consumed, O sons of Jacob. MALACHI 3:6 (NKJV)

> Let your light so shine before men that they may see your moral excellence and your praiseworthy, noble, and good deeds and recognize and honor and praise and glorify your Father Who is in heaven. MATTHEW 5:16 (AMP)

LIFE PURPOSE

Your life purpose has great importance and eternal impact. It is the pinnacle, the height of your existence and it should be obvious to all who encounter you. It is given to you by God Himself. Life purpose speaks to the reason for your existence. At its best, it becomes the central theme that surrounds your life. It encompasses all that you have dedicated your life to and you become known by it. Your life purpose should be condensed into a series of words describing you. Purpose is the quintessential reason why God created you.

It is from gaining an understanding of your purpose and fulfilling it that your life message is advanced.

THE CONTINUUM OF LIFE PURPOSE

There are four stages on the continuum of life purpose. Let's look at each stage.

Life Purpose Fulfilled

When your life purpose is fulfilled, your life will have these characteristics:

1. Highly developed in gifts, talents, and abilities
2. Ruling passion is fully incorporated in life endeavors
3. Operating in full understanding and application of motivational gifts (yours and others)
4. Life work is consistent with gifting and ruling passion
5. Fully developed in life service/ministry

6. Godly life message
7. God's greatness is manifested through your life

A person who has a fulfilled life purpose is not someone you find complaining about their job. They're not declaring "blue Mondays" or "thank God, it's Friday." Instead, they are so on fire for God and their ruling passion is so overwhelming in them, that they are excited to take on new assignments. When you have this attitude, the Lord can bless and increase you and cause prosperity to rest on you. It is only when your purpose is fulfilled that God can use you to heights untold and heights unknown.

Life Purpose Marginally Fulfilled

When your life purpose is only marginally fulfilled, your life will have these characteristics:

1. Somewhat developed in gifts, talents, and abilities
2. Ruling passion is known but not incorporated in life endeavors
3. Marginally developed in understanding and application of motivational gifts (yours and others)
4. Life work consistent with gifting but not guided by ruling passion
5. Inconsistent in life service/ministry
6. Life message may or may not be consistent with godly values
7. God's greatness is sporadically manifested in life

A person whose life purpose is marginally fulfilled is someone who is underdeveloped in their God-given gifts. You perform your job well, but your ruling passion is unfulfilled. You may have developed talents and skills that enable you to do your job well, but you know there is greatness on the inside of you that needs to be manifested in order for you to move into what God has called you to do. In other words, you may earn a good income and have a good life, but you still have an emptiness on the inside — a great sense of being unfulfilled. You will also be inconsistent in your actions. At times you will be faithful, and at other times you will not. God may bless you mightily every so often, but because of the inconsistency in your life, you take yourself out of position for consistent moves of God. This is why so many people in the body of Christ are waiting on a mighty move of God in their lives, but God is waiting on them to line themselves up according to His Word, so that He can bless them.

Life Purpose Hindered

When your life purpose is hindered, you feel great dissatisfaction with your life. You feel as though you are wandering through life aimlessly. Your life will have these characteristics:

1. Low or lacking development in gifts, talents, and/or abilities
2. Ruling passion is not incorporated in life endeavors and has become a frustration
3. Slightly developed or underdeveloped in the concept of motivational gift
4. Life work inconsistent with gifting and unrelated to ruling passion
5. Unable to effectively have a life service/ministry due to continuous emerging personal issues
6. Life message is unpredictable concerning godly values
7. God's greatness is once in a while manifested through your life

When your life purpose is hindered, you will be frustrated with your life. The job you perform is so against your ruling passion that it frustrates you tremendously. You may know what your motivational gift is, but you are not developing it. Thus, you are not glorifying God and you're hindering yourself from walking in God's best for your life.

If your life purpose is hindered, you are not consistent in what God has created you to do. Therefore His anointing will not rest on you at a very high level. You are out of the perfect will of God. You have been operating in His permissive will and He has dealt with you about it, yet you are not taking the necessary steps to get into your purpose. You will be frustrated and God cannot bless you. Grace and mercy are your cornerstones. Thank God for that, but you want to be under the spout where God's glory comes out.

Inconsistency abounds when your life purpose is hindered. You take ten steps forward on fire for God, but an obstacle arises and you take fifteen steps back. This causes inconsistency in your life message. People may see you on fire, giving God glory one day, and the next you are depressed. They don't know what they will hear when they speak to you. Yet, you can get on track — the Word says that you can do all things through Christ!

> I can do all things through Christ who strengthens me.
>
> PHILIPPIANS 4:13 (NKJV)

Life Purpose Perverted

When your life purpose is perverted, you are operating outside of God's will. You use your gifts and natural abilities for the wrong reasons. Your life has these characteristics:

1. Highly developed in talents and/or abilities, but use them for the wrong reasons
2. Ruling passion is not incorporated in life endeavors and has become an annoyance and creates an inner struggle
3. Completely undeveloped in the concept of motivational gift
4. Life work is either unethical or illegal
5. Corrupt motives make life service/ministry impure
6. Life message is ungodly and/or hypocritical
7. The work of Satan is manifested through your life

You can pervert what the Lord has given you when you use your gifts and abilities for ungodly purposes. When your life purpose is perverted, you *know* what is ethically and morally correct, but you make a decision to go against it.

In this stage, you do not know what your motivational gift is and you are not utilizing your God-given gifts and abilities the way the Lord intended. For example, twenty years ago, a local Detroit gang called Young Boys, Inc., gave rise to the mass manufacturing and selling of street drugs through children. They were likened to Henry Ford who gave rise to the mass production of automobiles.

Can you imagine what they could have done with that highly developed skill if used to the glory of God? God wants us to use our gifts to His glory and benefit. The drug dealers may make money, but they are deeply unsatisfied with their short and/or jail-ridden lives. There is a void in their lives that can only be filled by God. Those with perverted life purpose often have a shortened life span. You want to line up on God's side. He will bless you with a long, full, and satisfied life.

> With long life I will satisfy him, And show him My salvation.
>
> PSALM 91:16 (NKJV)

> So are the ways of everyone who is greedy for gain; it takes away the life of its owners.
>
> PROVERBS 1:19 (NKJV)

> He who is greedy for gain troubles his own house...
>
> PROVERBS 15:27A (NKJV)

HOW TO MATURE IN YOUR LIFE PURPOSE

Your life work and your life service/ministry equal your life purpose. Your purpose is a compilation of your work and service. If you do not get started early, you will be playing catch-up along the way. Yet God will redeem the time you have lost. As long as you get on track and stay focused, your latter years will be greater than your former.

> Though your beginning was small, Yet your latter end would increase abundantly. JOB 8:7 (NKJV)

It is important to mature and develop in understanding your God-given purpose. Here are some recommendations for maturing:

1. Do what God has called and gifted you to do

2. Be established in your life work
    a. Be an expert in your area of discipline

3. Be established in your life service/ministry
    a. Serve God
    b. Serve your family
    c. Serve your church
    d. Serve at your workplace
    e. Serve your community

4. Be an excellent example to others
    a. Spiritually strong
    b. Morally upstanding
    c. Full of integrity

5. Hobbies and interests
    a. Engage in activities that enhance your purpose
    b. Engage in activities that add to the quality of your life service/ministry
    c. Help others

6. Civic duty
    a. Vote for godly politicians and judges (where applicable) locally, state-wide, and nationally
    b. Exemplify excellent citizenship — statesmanship
    c. Pay your taxes
    d. Develop a greater good mentality
    e. Write letters and sign petitions to be a godly influence on your legislators and judges

7. Mentors (for your mentors and for you as a mentor)
    a. Be or have seasoned and developed individuals
    b. Associate with experts in your field of endeavor
    c. Help you maintain focus
    d. Help you hone your skills to a greater degree
    e. Provide constructive criticism
    f. Identify strengths and weaknesses
    g. Provide accountability

8. Volunteer time
    a. Make a positive difference (church work, charities)
    b. Work with seasoned professionals providing quality time and effort

9. Job training
    a. Seek continued education
    b. Keep current with industry changes
    c. Keep current with technological advances

10. Maturing in Your Purpose
    a. Branch out into diverse areas operating from your primary discipline and perfected base

Ultimately, maturing in your life purpose is key.

GOD EXPECTS GREATNESS FROM YOUR LIFE

God expects greatness from your life. This is why discovering and fulfilling your purpose is essential — it is absolutely vital to living a full, satisfied, and complete life.

The life of Jesus illustrates God's best for our lives. As a young child, Jesus sought the Lord about His life purpose. He studied, meditated, and applied the Word of God to His life. He operated in godly character. He spent time in prayer and allowed His life to be directed by the Spirit of God. This enabled Him to manifest His inner greatness in His life work, service, and ministry to the world. Thus, He was able to declare that He fulfilled His life purpose — He finished the work the Father had given Him to do.

> I have glorified You on earth. I have finished the work which You have given Me to do. JOHN 17:4 (NKJV)

Paul, the Apostle, said that he poured himself out as a drink offering and did what the Lord called him to do. He declared that there was a crown of righteousness awaiting him for he had fulfilled his God-ordained purpose. God wants the same for you!

> I have fought the good fight, I have finished the race, I have kept the faith. Finally, there is laid up for me the crown of righteousness, which the Lord, the righteous Judge, will give to me on that Day, and not to me only but also to all who have loved His appearing. 2 TIMOTHY 4:7-8 (NKJV)

When you please God, He will bless your going in and coming out. He will bless you in your storehouses. He will bless you and the work of your hands. He will open His good treasure to you when you are in your purpose.

However, when you are not in your purpose, you will struggle. You will be unsatisfied and unfulfilled, feeling that there must be more to life than what you are experiencing.

The ways of the Lord are pleasing and glorious. God wants you to have a full, satisfied, and long life, and He will bless you if you will walk in your purpose. It is our prayer that you will get on your face before God and make a decision to get into your purpose and walk it out.

God expects you to walk in the greatness He has called you to — and so do we!

A PROPHETIC MESSAGE ON THE SPIRIT OF CREATIVITY

At the taping of the *How to Discover Your Purpose in 10 Days* television show, Minister Catherine B. Eagan shared the following prophetic message:

> *We are going into an age where God will raise people up with high levels of creativity. God is going to begin to renew people by giving them ideas and witty inventions. We are beyond the manufacturing age; it has moved to India and China. God will begin to bring creativity to those people who are in their purpose, so they may run with the vision and dominate to the glory of God.*
>
> *You hear great economists such as Alan Greenspan saying that we are beyond the Information Age. We are in the intellectual property age – the age of creativity and invention. Therefore, as a believer, it is critically important to know that you are called of God to enter into a level of creativity unknown.*

This time will be greater than any time before, so you need to understand your purpose at a higher level than you ever have before. As you enter into your purpose and receive from the Spirit of God and walk out your purpose to the glory of God, God will begin to embellish you and bless you. God will then be able to raise you up causing people to call you a delightsome land; and just as with Joseph, people will declare that truly the hand of the Lord is upon you.

We expect to see great inventions, industry dominators, and see young people ruling and reigning in Christ Jesus in this life. We expect to see the whole world changed because they have heard this revolutionary message and hearkened unto the Word of the Lord, receiving it with gladness and have acted upon it to the glory of God.

10

DAY TEN

Fulfilling the Greatness Within

CONCLUSION POINTS

You have been fearfully and wonderfully made in the image of God. He knew exactly what He was doing when He formed you and fashioned you after Himself. He created you with a purpose — an awesome destiny.

There is greatness locked inside of you, and it is only when you begin to operate within your purpose that you will fulfill your destiny.

Your ruling passion that the Lord placed within you yearns for manifestation, and it is God's best that it is expressed through your life work and life service/ministry.

The combination of your life work and life service/ministry equal your life purpose. Your life purpose reflects the very essence of your being and it has eternal impact. It has been given to you by God and should be obvious to all who encounter you — defining your life message.

It is vital to discover and operate in your God-ordained purpose. By doing so, your life work, life service/ministry, and life message will reflect the inner greatness God has placed within you.

10

DAY TEN

Fulfilling the Greatness Within

KEY POINTS

- You were fearfully and wonderfully made in the very image and likeness of God Himself.

- God has placed inner greatness within you that yearns for expression. It is reflected in your motivational gift, your ruling passion, and your natural gifts and abilities.

- God created you to fulfill a great and mighty purpose on earth — you were formed with an awesome destiny.

- It is only when you operate in your purpose that your life has true significance and meaning.

- Work is a gift from God and He expects you to dedicate yourself to the life work that He has called you to fulfill.

- You are called to spend time adding to the lives of others through your life service/ministry. You minister to others through your relationship with God and your family, your church, your workpace, your civic duty and community service.

- Your life message evolves and changes as you grow and mature in your life work. It is the conscious or subconscious statement of the very essence of your being. You have a God-ordained purpose, but your life message is what you choose to live.

PRAYERFUL REFLECTION

Dear Heavenly Father, I thank You and give You praise and glory that before the foundation of the world, You knew who I would be. Thank You Lord for loving me so very much that I would be created with a purpose, fully equipped with everything I need to fulfill Your purpose on the inside of me. I thank You gracious Father, that you would bring parents, mentors, early jobs, hobbies, opportunities, and exposure into my life to allow me to blossom and manifest the greatness that You placed inside of me.

Thank you Lord for the blood of Jesus that protects me and keeps me from hurt, harm, and danger. Thank You Lord for the blood that cleanses me and washes off every obstacle that tries to come against the work that You have planned for me to perform.

I thank You Lord God that You have given me a motivational gift and that You have uniquely equipped me to grow and develop in the gifts that You have placed inside of me. Thank You that You have called me to greatness because You are great and I am made in Your likeness and image. For this, I give You praise and glory.

I am ever grateful to You God for giving me a great destiny. I purpose to walk this destiny out and live a legacy that is glorifying and pleasing to You, that I may be a blessing to others. I will never take for granted that You have given me a purpose and I commit to walk my purpose out. I love You Lord and will bless Your holy name forever. In Jesus' name and by His blood, I pray. Amen.

DAY 10: ACTION PLAN

Please use the *Prayers and Daily Journal* or the *Self-Assessment Workbook* as needed to complete the following items in your action plan.

1. Pray and thank God for creating you with a specific purpose.

2. Write out your life purpose in your *Prayers and Daily Journal.*

3. In your *Prayers and Daily Journal,* state your present life message. Also, state what you want your life message to be in the future.

4. Create and write a vision statement in your Prayers and Daily

Journal of what God has placed on your heart to accomplish in your lifetime.

5. Prayerfully reflect on how you currently spend your time. Prayerfully reflect on what adjustments need to be made to ensure that your time is being spent most effectively to the glory of God.

6. Seek the Lord's direction on how to move along the continuum of life purpose so that you will get into the stage of Life Purpose Fulfilled.

7. Identify ways you can become highly developed in your purpose and list them in your *Prayers and Daily Journal.*

8. Spend time in prayer and ask the Lord to reveal to you the areas you need to focus on to mature and develop in your purpose. Write them in your *Prayers and Daily Journal.* Work hard to be faithful.

9. Make a decision to be excellent in all of your areas of life service, including your:
    a. Relationship with God
    b. Family
    c. Church
    d. Workplace
    e. Community
    f. Civic duty

IF YOU DO NOT KNOW THE LORD, GIVE YOUR HEART TO JESUS TODAY

The Word of God says in Romans 10:9-10, that "if you shall confess with your mouth the Lord Jesus, and believe in your heart that God has raised Him from the dead, you will be saved. For with the heart one believes unto righteousness, and with the mouth confession is made unto salvation."

If you do not know the Lord as your Savior, you can recite this simple prayer of salvation: I believe Jesus Christ is the Son of God, that He carried my sins for me, and that He died on the cross at Calvary. He was put in a grave, but I believe He is risen and alive right now. Lord Jesus, come into my heart and save me now. I believe in my heart, therefore I confess with my mouth that Jesus Christ is now my personal Lord and Savior. Thank you Lord for saving me now. In Jesus' name, I pray. Amen.

(If you prayed this prayer, congratulations! We are so very excited for you. We want to e-mail you a free e-book to help you on your Christian journey. Please contact us at info@eaganbooks.com.)

WORKPLACE
WISDOM

Share Your Personal Testimony with Us

We would love to hear about the awesome things that the Lord has done in your life as a result of your reading and applying the principles we have shared in this book. Let us know how this book has affected you and what other information you would like us to share in future material at info@eaganbooks.com.

We also invite you to send us your e-mail address, so that we may send you a complimentary copy of The Eagan Report on a periodic basis. For more information, visit our web site: www.eaganbooks.com.

God bless you!

Remember, God is expecting greatness in your life!

PURPOSE

ENDNOTES

Endnotes

1. Dr. Myles Munroe, *In Pursuit of Purpose* (Shippensburg, PA: Destiny Image Publishers, 1992), 5-6.

2. *Forbes*, "The World's Richest People," http://www.forbes.com/maserati/billionaires2004/bill04land.html (accessed August 11, 2004).

3. Microsoft, "Microsoft Reports Fourth Quarter Earnings," http://www.microsoft.com/presspass/press/2003/jul03/07-17q03-4earningspr.asp (accessed August, 11 2004).

4. Microsoft, "William H. Gates Chairman and Chief Software Architect, Microsoft Corporation," http://www.microsoft.com/bill gates/bio.asp (accessed August 11, 2004).

5. John Maxwell, *Thinking for a Change* (New York: Warner Books, 2003), 99-100.

6. *American Dictionary of the English Language*, Noah Webster 1828. (San Francisco: Foundation for American Christian Education, 1967, 1995), s.v. "Education."

7. *Investor's Business Daily*, "He Made Self-Fulfilled Profits," http://biz.yahoo.com/ibd/040719/lands_1.html (accessed August 16, 2004).

8. PBS, *American Experience, The Rockefellers*, http://www.pbs.org/wgbh/amex/rockefellers/peopleevents/p_rock_jsr.html (accessed August 16, 2004).

9. Ron Chernow, *Titan: The Life of John D. Rockefeller, Sr.* (New York: Random House, Inc., 1998), 55.

10. *Ibid*, 61.

11. William Thayer, *Gaining Favor with God and Man* (Bulverde, TX: Mantle Ministries, 1989), 323.

12. The Divorce Center, Inc., "Divorce Rates in the United States," http://www.divorcecenter.org/faqs/stats.htm (accessed August 11, 2004).

13. Patrick Lagan and Caroline Harlow. "Child Rape Victims, 1992." Washington, DC: Bureau of Justice Statistics, U.S. Department of Justice, 1994.

14. National Center for Victims of Crime and Crime Victims Research and Treatment. "Rape in America: A Report to the Nation." Arlington, VA: National Center for Victims of Crime and Crime Victims Research and Treatment Center, 1992.

15. David Lisak, "The Psychological Impact of Sexual Abuse: Content Analysis of Interviews with Male Survivors," *Journal of Traumatic Stress* 7(4): 525-548.

16. Federal Bureau of Investigation. "Uniform Crime Reports for the United States: 1999." Washington, DC: U.S. Government Printing Office, 2000.

17. Southeast Missouri Network Against Sexual Violence, "Adult Sexual Assault," http://www.semonasv.org/ADULTSEXUALAS SAULT.htm (accessed August 11, 2004).

18. Substance Abuse and Mental Health Services Administration, an agency of the U.S. Department of Health and Human Services, http://www.samhsa.gov/index.aspx (accessed August, 11 2004).

19. *The Random House Dictionary of the English Language*, 2nd ed., s.v. "Nature."

20. Thomas Stanley, *The Millionaire Mind* (Kansas City, MO: Andrews McMeel Publishing, 2000).

Other Resources

If you enjoyed *How to Discover Your Purpose in 10 Days*, we also recommend other resources by Dr. J. Victor and Catherine B. Eagan.

DOMINATING MONEY: PERSONAL FINANCIAL INTELLIGENCE

- *Dominating Money, 16-Set Series*
- *10 Keys to Dominating Money, 2-Set Series*
- *Eliminating Debt, 2-Set Series*
- *Budgeting, 2-Set Series*

ANOINTED FOR WORK: USING THE TOOLS FROM SUNDAY TO SUCCEED ON MONDAY

- *Anointed for Work, 14-Set Series*

DOMINATING BUSINESS: HOW TO PROSPER ON YOUR JOB

- *Dominating Business, 16-Set Series*
- *Servant Leadership, 2-Set Series*
- *What Type of Businessperson Would Jesus Have Been? 2-Set Series*
- *Your Work Matters to God, 2-Set Series*

HOW TO DETERMINE YOUR MOTIVATIONAL GIFT: LEARN HOW GOD WIRED YOU

- *How to Determine Your Motivational Gift, 15-Set Series*

HOW TO DISCOVER YOUR PURPOSE IN 10 DAYS: GOD'S PATH TO A FULL AND SATISFIED LIFE

- *How to Discover Your Purpose in 10 Days, 12-CD Series*
- *How to Discover Your Purpose in 10 Days, 12-DVD Series*

HOME-STUDY COURSES AVAILABLE

- *Dominating Money*
- *Dominating Business*
- *Anointed for Work*

WORKPLACE STUDY MATERIALS

- *Word @ Work, Volume I*
- *Word @ Work, Volume II*

WORKPLACE WISDOM INSTITUTE

www.workplacewisdominstitute.com

What Is the Workplace Wisdom Institute?

Workplace Wisdom Institute is a systematic series of eight, 8-week online courses designed to teach you how to practically apply biblical principles and the Word of God in the workplace. The goal is to encourage the character and excellence of Christ in the workplace. Christians should be the most profitable, highly-successful and fully-satisfied people at work.

Who Should Take These Courses?

These courses are recommended for working people, entrepreneurs, business professionals, managers, supervisors and all people in the workplace from the CEO to every level; and anyone called to practice the principles of God in the workplace, namely every Christian.

COURSE OFFERINGS

How to Prosper on Your Job

Find out what God's Word says about prospering and increasing on your job.

How to Take God's Power to Your Job

Learn how to be more powerful than your non-Christian counterparts in every situation.

How to Determine Your Motivational Gift
Learn how God wired you and understand why you and others have different views.

Dominating Money — Personal Finance
Areas of focus include budgeting, credit, debt, cash flow, estate planning, and more!

The Character of Success
Increase productivity, profitability, and teamwork to excel to the glory of God.

Godly Leadership and Ethics
Integrate highly successful strategies to maximize the gifts and talents of your team.

Dominating Money — In Business
Learn how to start and manage businesses and the principles of millionaire thinking.

How to Terminate Conflict
Neutralize conflict completely with superiors, co-workers, and others.

How to Discover Your Purpose in 10 Days
Discover your unique, God-given, life assignment so that you may live a full and satisfied life and be in the perfect will of God.

For on-line course information, please visit
www.workplacewisdominstitute.com.

WORKPLACE
WISDOM